"In this engaging and highly readable book for teens, Amy Sa[...] mindfulness activities, questions to reflect on, and nuggets of wise guidance. Reading this book and trying the suggested activities is like having a kind and wise friend holding your hand, step-by-step, down the road to less unnecessary stress and greater well-being!"

—**Dzung X. Vo, MD**, author of *The Mindful Teen*

"This book is a treasure to explore and absorb. It speaks directly to teens in a clear, respectful, and compassionate way, and invites curiosity and engagement with lightness and without pretense. Amy Saltzman is a gifted teacher of mindfulness and life, and she invites the teen reader to consider what the practice of mindfulness has to offer, to let each reader come to his or her own conclusion about their experience with the practice, and does it with a light touch informed by a deep practice and dedication to the potential of mindfulness. *A Still Quiet Place for Teens* offers a time-proven program that has helped youth of all ages for many years now, and to have a book dedicated to sharing this amazing program with others is a true gift to all who choose to receive it."

—**Steven D. Hickman, PsyD**, clinical psychologist and executive director at the University of California, San Diego Center for Mindfulness; and associate clinical professor in the UC San Diego departments of psychiatry and family and preventive medicine

"With wisdom and compassion, Amy Saltzman invites teens to look squarely at themselves and their relationships, then offers understandings and tools to transform both. Don't be fooled by the title. This is a book for everyone who has ever been a teen."

—**Richard Brady, MS**, cofounder of the Mindfulness in Education Network

"If you want less stress, more peace, and an easier time navigating the challenging years of adolescence, read this book. Discover and build the wisdom within yourself in Saltzman's *A Still Quiet Place for Teens*."

—**Mark Bertin, MD**, developmental pediatrician and author of
Mindful Parenting for ADHD

"Clear, accessible, and to the point, Amy Saltzman's worksheets deftly translate her years of experience working with youth and supporting mindfulness educators into something every parent, teacher, or clinician can use to share mindfulness with the teenagers in their lives."

—**Susan Kaiser Greenland**, author of *The Mindful Child*, and cofounder
of Inner Kids

"Amy Saltzman has offered yet another invaluable resource for teens dealing with struggles of adolescent life, from test-anxiety to trauma. This workbook offers practical, easy-to-read activities and practices that are innovative and accessible to teens of all different sorts of backgrounds. These time-tested mindfulness practices—from easily remembered acronyms to innovative ways for understanding and practicing mindfulness—can help teens deal with the struggles of daily life and become aware of the power they have inside themselves. Highly recommended for teens, parents, educators, and therapists."

—**Sam Himelstein, PhD**, psychologist at the Alameda County Juvenile
Justice Center, founder of the Center for Adolescent Studies, and
coauthor of *Mindfulness-Based Substance Abuse Treatment for Adolescents*

"Amy Saltzman has again provided the world with a wonderful contribution, revealing how teens can learn a no-nonsense way to reduce overwhelming stress and bring more focus, health, and resilience into their lives. What is also in it for you as teen, or for anyone who might care to learn from this magnificent teacher, is a self-knowledge and set of social and emotional skills that will last a lifetime. You will learn from a kind and thoughtful teacher how to build these same qualities in yourself. What are you waiting for?"

—**Daniel J. Siegel, MD**, author of *The Mindful Brain*, *The Mindful Therapist*, *The Developing Mind*, *Brainstorm*, and *Mindsight*; executive director of the Mindsight Institute; founding codirector of the UCLA Mindful Awareness Research Center; and clinical professor at the David Geffen School of Medicine at UCLA

"Amy Saltzman's workbook is an incredible way for you to learn skills for staying calm and present through any challenging situations life will eventually throw your way—in school, at parties, or on the field. Mindfulness doesn't need to be complicated, time consuming, or weird, and Saltzman can help you fit it into all of the important aspects of your life. I look forward to sharing this gift with my own teenaged clients and students."

—**Christopher Willard, PsyD**, author of *Child's Mind* and *Mindfulness for Teen Anxiety*

"In this book, Dr. Amy talks about many of the things I learned in my one-on-one sessions with her. It was a great refresher on my mindfulness skills, and I think this book will successfully lead many other teens into living mindfully."

—**Francesca**, age twelve, nationally competitive diver

"I love Dr. Amy's view of mindfulness and loving-kindness as skills which you can learn, practice, and hone—and that the 'gift of mindfulness' is something you can always give yourself, even in the span of just a few breaths. The book gives clear, simple, and relatable instructions and activities that ease you into mindfulness practice. I really, truly enjoyed *A Still Quiet Place for Teens*; Dr. Amy's voice comes through so sincerely. I know the book is addressed to teens but I still feel like I personally got a lot out of it, and I think pretty much anyone I know, at any age, would benefit from reading the book and following along with the activities."

—**Cora**, age twenty-one, first-year master's degree student at the University of California, Santa Barbara's Bren School of Environmental Science and Management

"I enjoyed and found helpful many of the activities in this workbook. For example, I especially enjoyed the activity where I made different facial expressions to see how that affected my emotions. I noticed it made me feel calmer. The book helped me understand mindfulness better. I recommend this to other teens!"

—**Jessica**, ninth grader

"It was good. I enjoyed all of the activities and the writing was interesting. It helped me feel better about my pain. Good job!"

—**Kaela**, seventh grader

"The workbook is very calming. The exercises are easy to apply and very handy after a stressful day."

—**Bilel**, age eleven

a still quiet place for teens

a mindfulness workbook to ease stress & difficult emotions

AMY SALTZMAN, MD

Instant Help Books
An Imprint of New Harbinger Publications, Inc.

Publisher's Note

Distributed in Canada by Raincoast Books

Copyright © 2016 by Amy Saltzman
        Instant Help Books
        An Imprint of New Harbinger Publications, Inc.
        5674 Shattuck Avenue
        Oakland, CA 94609
        www.newharbinger.com

Cover design by Amy Shoup; Edited by Brady Kahn; Acquired by Tesilya Hanauer; Illustrations by Kristin Wiens

---

Library of Congress Cataloging-in-Publication Data on file

Printed in the United States of America

18   17   16

10 9 8 7 6 5 4 3 2 1   First printing

With boundless gratitude for

My beloved mentor, Georgina Lindsey

My amazing and ordinary children, Jason and Nicole

My loving husband, Eric

My dear mindfulness friends and colleagues

The wise, brave teens whom I have had the privilege to serve

And, ultimately, for the Still Quiet Place

Contents

part 4: feelings and unpleasant events

part 5: emotions, responding vs. reacting

part 6: responding and communicating

part 7: choice and kindness

part 8: the end of the out-breath

Welcome and Congrats!

Hi, and congratulations! I realize it may sound crazy, and by cracking open this book and beginning to read, you have taken the first step toward decreasing your stress and increasing your happiness. As your first mindfulness exercise, simply notice the thoughts and feelings that appear as you reread this sentence: "By cracking open this book and beginning to read, you have taken the first step toward decreasing your stress and increasing your happiness." Maybe you feel a sense of hopefulness or relief, like *Oh good. There's something I can do to be kind to and support myself.* Maybe you feel doubt and resistance, like *There's no way that just reading a book can help me with my problems.* Take a moment and just be really honest with yourself about what you're thinking and feeling...

Excellent! You've just done your first mindfulness practice!

About now, you may be wondering exactly what mindfulness is. Mindfulness is paying attention here and now, with kindness and curiosity, so that we can choose our behavior.

Let's break that definition down. "Paying attention here and now" means not dwelling on the past or worrying about the future but paying attention to what's actually happening in this moment. We do this "with kindness and curiosity." Often we are incredibly hard on ourselves. We tend to see only where we've "made a mistake" or "screwed up." With practice, we can learn to be kinder to ourselves and curious about our experience instead of judging and criticizing ourselves. And finally, "so that we can choose our behavior": when we bring our kind and curious attention to our thoughts and feelings, to the sensations in our bodies, and to the people and circumstances in our lives, then we have all the information we need to make choices that allow us to live our lives and fulfill our dreams as best we can.

So again, pause here and notice what you're thinking and feeling. Maybe you're thinking *Cool! I'll give it a try.* Or maybe you're thinking *She doesn't know anything about me and my life; there's no way this can help me.* Whatever you're thinking and feeling is absolutely fine. There is nothing you need to change or fix.

Just so you know, I've shared the practices in this book with all types of teens: teens dealing with ordinary everyday stresses of living in our fast-paced, media-driven world; teens dealing with intense parents, high expectations, and extreme pressure to get into a "good" college; teens from low-income, violent communities; teens living with ADHD, anxiety, depression, or eating disorders; teens who have been in gangs, gotten pregnant, been suspended, or gone to jail; teens whose families are going through a divorce or dealing with a serious illness or financial hardship; teens using drugs, cutting, and engaging in other self-harming behaviors, including thinking about or attempting suicide. So whether you're failing math, fighting with your parents, dealing with more intense issues, or just want to have some skills to deal with ordinary everyday stress, this book is for *you*.

As you read, it may be helpful to know that the ellipses (...) indicate a pause, a time to slow down and *really* allow yourself to feel or experience the full effect of the suggestions in the practices. Some phrases in this workbook will be repeated over and over so that eventually they will live in your mind and heart and become a part of your life. Many themes will be presented several times in slightly different ways so that you can find what works best for you.

The book has eight parts, following the format of my eight-week in-person course, "Still Quiet Place: Mindfulness in Daily Life." I suggest that you do one part a week for eight weeks. The exercises and ideas build on each other, so it's best if you do them in order. That said, if you find yourself curious about a particular exercise title, then flip to that page and learn what you can. If a chapter later in the book builds on earlier material, I will let you know that at the beginning of the chapter and refer you to the related material.

There are four types of elements in this book:

Basic concepts: As the name suggests, these chapters present basic concepts that will support you in developing a mindfulness practice and using it in your everyday life.

Mindful practices: These exercises will be the core of your mindfulness practice. You'll benefit from doing them *repeatedly*, so for most of them, I provide guided audio, available at http://www.newharbinger.com/33766. (See the back of the book for information on how to access the downloads.) Most of the teens I work with like to load these practices onto their phones; that way they have the practices easily accessible when they want to use them, whether to help deal with a specific challenge or to just chill out.

Reflections: These exercises allow you to explore your experience with the mindful practices. They'll help you see how mindfulness is bringing kind and curious attention to your experiences; this is different from always being calm or blissed out. (We'll return to this idea later.) As you respond to the reflection prompts, I encourage you to go slowly and be brave and specific. Do your best to discover what's true for you, how you *really* think, feel, and behave. The more real you can be with yourself, the more you will benefit in your daily life.

Activities: These exercises are short, simple, paper-and-pencil activities that will help you understand mindfulness and see how it applies to your life.

Doing the exercises in this book will give you useful skills for eliminating some of the difficulties in your life, facing the challenges that remain, and enjoying more moments of peace and ease. The catch is that to develop these skills, you need to actually *do* the mindful practices. I encourage you to do each of the practices at least once.

There may be some practices that you find unusual or difficult, and over time, you may find these same practices to be extremely helpful, precisely because they're helping you develop new and needed skills. With patience, persistence, and a sense of humor, you will learn which practices are the most helpful to you and which you want to keep doing.

Here is what one tenth grader wrote about his experience with mindfulness, misspellings and all.

> *I have taken some classes this pass Fridays, and they have really helped me not just in school but in my personal life. With this class I have been able to control my anger and found technics to rest and be in peace with myself.*

Welcome. Now you too can sit back and rest.

taking a rest, taking a breath

In the beginning of this section, I invite you to *rest*, to allow yourself to slow down and simply take some time for yourself. After you have rested, you can learn a bit about the scientific evidence that shows that mindfulness can help you reduce stress and live a happier life. Then you will be introduced to a variety of mindful listening practices; these practices will increase your ability to hear sounds, music, and, most importantly, yourself. Overall, this section will serve as an introduction and foundation for your mindfulness practice. So sit back and *rest*.

chapter 1

Practice:
Rest

This first practice will allow you to just rest and chill out for a few minutes. It is a short and simple way to take a break from the worries and stresses of teen life. Downloadable audio for this practice is available at http://www.newharbinger .com/33766. (You may want to take a few minutes right now to download all of the recorded practices, including this one, so you can simply close your eyes and listen to each practice when you come to it.)

As you begin, it will be helpful to find a quiet protected place where you won't be disturbed—in a corner of the school library, outside on a bench or by a tree, or in your bedroom. Once you become more familiar with mindful resting, you'll be able to do it anywhere—in a noisy classroom, on a crowded train, or before an audition, job interview, or sports competition.

If you haven't downloaded the audio yet, I encourage you to do so now. If you are choosing to read, read through the following instructions, *slowly*. The instructions suggest closing your eyes if you feel comfortable doing so. Of course, if you are reading, you won't be able to do that until after you've read the practice. So if you're choosing to learn this practice by reading it, you may want to read a paragraph, then close your eyes and slowly follow the instructions in that paragraph, then read the next paragraph, and so on. As you read and practice, let the *feeling* of rest wash over you.

Give it a rest. For the next few minutes, give it a rest—all of it—homework, your parents, the hallway gossip, your inner gossip, the next new thing...let everything be exactly the way it is...and rest.

Let your body rest. If you feel comfortable, allow your eyes to close. If not, focus on a neutral spot in front of you. Feel your body supported by the chair, the couch, the bed, or the floor. Allow the muscles in your body and your face to rest. Maybe even let out a long slow sigh…

Let your attention rest on the breath…the rhythm of the breath in the belly. Feel the belly expand with each in-breath and release with each out-breath…narrowing your attention to the rhythm of the breath and allowing everything else to fade into the background…breathing, resting…nowhere to go, nothing to do, no one to be, nothing to prove.

Feel the entire in-breath, from the very first sip all the way through to where the breath is still…and the entire out-breath, from the first whisper all the way through to where the breath is still… Now see if you can let your attention rest in the Still Quiet Place between the in-breath and the out-breath… And rest again in the still space between the out-breath and the in-breath…

Breathing, resting, being… This is more than enough…just hanging out with the breath and the stillness…

Feeling the stillness and quietness that is always inside of you…

And when your attention wanders, which it will, gently return it to the experience of breathing—feeling the rhythm of the breath in the belly…

Choosing to rest. Choosing to focus your attention on the breath. Allowing things to be just as they are…allowing yourself to be exactly as you are… There's nothing to change, or fix, or improve…

Breathing and resting. Resting and breathing.

As this practice session comes to a close, you may want to remember that in our fast-paced, media-driven world, resting is a radical act. With practice, you can learn to breathe and rest anytime, anywhere: when you're putting on your shoes…when you're struggling in class…when you're hanging out with friends…even when you're arguing with someone… This kind of resting and breathing is especially helpful when you're nervous, depressed, bored, or angry.

Now that you have finished reading, please *give yourself permission to rest*; take three to five minutes to simply rest with your breath as described.

chapter 2

Reflection:
What Was It Like to Rest?

Take some time now to reflect on your experience of resting.

Were you able to rest? Circle one: Yes.   No.   Sort of.

Whether you were able to rest or not, bring your kind and curious attention to your experience:

How did your mind feel?

_____

_____

_____

How did your body feel?

_____

_____

_____

How did your heart feel?

_____

_____

_____

What helped you rest?

_____

_____

_____

What did you find challenging about resting?

_____

_____

_____

Because most of us are used to being on the go and thinking about all the things we have to do, resting may feel like a huge relief, or it may feel a bit unusual or even uncomfortable. However you experienced resting is *absolutely fine*. With practice, resting in the stillness and quietness will become easier.

Sometimes when you sit down to rest, you may discover that your mind is racing, that you're feeling sad or angry, or that your body is fidgety. Noticing these experiences with kindness and curiosity is *mindfulness*. Images on social media, in the movies, on TV, and even on billboards give the impression that being mindful means always being calm, peaceful, and blissed out. It doesn't! Being mindful means simply being aware of whatever is happening here and now. So if your body is exhausted, your mood is excited, or your mind is bored, and you're aware of your experience, you're being mindful.

Again, there's nothing you need to change or fix. It's more than enough to simply bring your kind and curious attention to your experience in the moment, the here and now.

chapter 3

Activity:
What Stresses You Out?

As human beings, we all have many sources of stress. As a teen, you have some unique sources of stress. What are your primary sources of stress? Take a look at the following words, and circle any that are sources of stress for you. If you have sources of stress that aren't mentioned here, feel free to write them in.

FAMILY MEMBER

parents

mom

sister

tryouts

dad

history

college admission

stepparent

brother

BOSS

tests

theater

auditions

homework

music

science

job

ENGLISH

boyfriend

coach

foreign language

coworkers

girlfriend

bullying

math

money

a fear

discrimination

sports

a secret

body image

friends

BODY WEIGHT

a mistake

AN ILLNESS

violence

a diagnosis

harassment

crime

In the next activity, a few key questions will help you mindfully consider small, medium, and big stressors in your life. Here's an example using a small stressor from my own life.

Small stressor: *My "homework," specifically doing bookkeeping*

How does my body feel when I think about this stressor?

Heavy, slow, with a dull ache at my temples

What are my thoughts about this stressor?

Ugh. I hate bookkeeping. I don't want to do it. I wish I hadn't procrastinated. I wish it were finished.

What emotions appear? How do I feel when I think about this stressor?

Irritated. Agitated. Impatient. Annoyed.

Now, write down three of your own stressors (which you circled earlier)—one small, one medium, and one large stressor—and, for each one, ask yourself the following series of questions. As you do this activity, practice bringing kindness and curiosity to your experience, and remember that in this moment there is nothing else you need to do.

Small stressor: _____

How does my body feel when I think about this stressor?

_____

_____

What are my thoughts about this stressor?

_____

_____

What emotions appear? How do I feel when I think about this stressor?

_____

_____

Medium stressor: _____

How does my body feel when I think about this stressor?

_____

_____

What are my thoughts about this stressor?

_____

_____

What emotions appear? How do I feel when I think about this stressor?

_____

_____

Large stressor: _____

How does my body feel when I think about this stressor?

_____

_____

What are my thoughts about this stressor?

_____

_____

What emotions appear? How do I feel when I think about this stressor?

_____

_____

Take a moment to acknowledge yourself. It requires courage to slow down and look directly at the things that you find stressful. I'm sure that, like most human beings, you wish you had a magic wand that could make your stressors disappear. And if it were that easy, you would have already gotten rid of your stressors, and there would be no need for this book. So while mindfulness won't make your stressors disappear, it will teach you new ways of dealing with them, and over time this will make your life more peaceful and joyful. Again, if you are thinking, *Mindfulness may be great for other people, but it can't help me*, read on. As you read, do your best to open your mind and heart to the possibility that mindfulness can help you. Then try it, and decide for yourself based on your experience.

chapter 4

Basic Concept:
The Benefits of Mindfulness

Mindfulness has been scientifically proven to have many benefits. Here are just a few:

* Decreasing stress

* Decreasing negative emotions

* Decreasing anger and behavior problems

* Decreasing anxiety in general and test anxiety in particular

* Decreasing depression

* Decreasing ADHD symptoms

* Increasing attention

* Increasing the ability to calm yourself

* Increasing self-esteem and self-compassion

* Increasing the ability to care for yourself and others

* Increasing social skills

* Increasing sleep quality

* Increasing a sense of calmness, relaxation, and self-acceptance

And studies using functional magnetic resonance imaging (fMRI), which produces images of the brain in action, have shown that people who practice mindfulness for eight weeks experience actual changes in the brain:

* Decreased gray-matter density in the amygdala, a part of the brain that plays an important role in signaling anxiety and stress

* Increased gray-matter density in the hippocampus, an area of the brain that's important for learning and memory

* Increased gray-matter density in the temporal-parietal junction, an area of the brain that's associated with self-awareness, compassion, and introspection

The take-home message is this: just as physical training strengthens the body, mindfulness training strengthens the mind. So if you want a mind that's better able to deal with the stresses of daily life, keep reading and practicing.

chapter 5

Basic Concept:
The Importance of Support

Mindfulness is a powerful tool, and it can provide all the benefits listed in chapter 4, if you commit to doing the practices. However, sometimes life is so intense that mindfulness alone is not enough. If you're dealing with major depression, severe anxiety, or any significant difficulty in your life, I encourage you to continue practicing mindfulness *and* to also seek additional support from a parent, wise and caring friend, school counselor, religious elder, therapist, or psychiatrist. There are some things no one should have to face alone. And there is no secret or burden that isn't made lighter by sharing it with another kind and compassionate human being. Your heart will know whom to ask for comfort and support.

chapter 6

Activity:
How Do You Know When People Are Listening?

When you talk to people, such as your parents, friends, teachers, brothers, sisters, classmates, or coaches, do you feel they're really listening?

Circle one: Yes.   No.   Sometimes.

Answer the following questions to discover how you know when people are really listening.

Where is their attention? _____

_____

Where are their eyes? _____

How do their facial expressions show that they're listening?

_____

_____

_____

How do their bodies show that they're listening?

_____

_____

_____

What is the rhythm or feeling of their speech and actions?

_____

_____

_____

_____

For me, when people are really listening, I can feel that they are being mindful. Their attention is with me, in the here and now. Their eyes are focused on me. Their face is kind, open, and curious. Their body is relaxed and at ease. Their speech and actions are slow and steady.

chapter 7

Practice:
Listening to Sounds

There are many ways to practice mindful listening. Let's start with listening to sounds.

After you read this paragraph, close your eyes and just listen. Really listen to all the sounds around you: sounds nearby...sounds farther away...the sounds of your breath...even the sound of your heartbeat. If your mind wanders from listening— and it will—use the next sound to return your attention to listening. Simply sit and listen for three to five minutes. You can set the timer on your phone, or after a few minutes, you can just use the next sound you hear to end your listening session.

chapter 8

Practice:
Listening to Music

For this practice, put on some music and crank up the volume! You might play your favorite song: hip hop, pop, rock, blues, jazz, classical, country—it doesn't matter. You could even put on a song that you hate. Whatever you choose, play the music and really *listen*.

Listen with your whole body, not just your ears. If you feel like it, let the music move you. Feel the beat, give yourself over to the rhythm, and bring your full attention to the music and the movement. Don't worry about getting it right: you can sit still, tap your toes, or dance wildly. *Hear* the music with your whole body.

Notice any thoughts of embarrassment or shyness, or thoughts like *This is ridiculous*. They're just thoughts.

Notice any feelings that are released: anger, joy, sadness…

Feel your body. Feel its aliveness.

Listen to the music and notice thoughts and the emotions moving through you.

And when the song comes to an end, notice the effects of really listening to music with your whole body.

chapter 9

Practice:
Listening to Yourself

It can be very helpful to take a few minutes each day to listen to yourself, just pausing to check in and offer yourself the same kindness and wisdom you'd offer a good friend. You can do this as you walk to class, sit down for lunch, shower, whatever. Just take a moment to sincerely ask yourself these questions:

What's up?

No really, what's up?

How am I feeling in this moment?

Is there something I'm really excited about?

Is there anything getting me down?

Am I feeling happy, sad, angry, stressed, tired, hungry...?

Is there a secret that I'm keeping?

Are there any changes I want to make?

Is there anything I can do to take care of myself?

This simple practice of checking in can really help you care for yourself. Maybe it would be helpful to get some exercise, take a break, buckle down and get some homework done, have a snack, call a friend, put on some tunes, or do a mindfulness practice, like Rest (chapter 1), or the Befriending Feelings practice (chapter 24).

Perhaps there is something bigger to be addressed. Are you feeling overwhelmed and that it would be best for you to drop one of your courses? Do you want to be brave and ask that certain someone out? Do you want to stop playing soccer and try out for the musical? Do you need additional support?

When we're busy and running on automatic, we're often unaware of how we're really feeling. And when we're unaware of how we're feeling, we often make poor choices—saying something that we regret, acting out, procrastinating, giving up, picking a fight, or just doing what we have always done because it is what we have always done…

So take a few moments every day to listen to yourself with kindness and curiosity. This will make it easier for you to *choose* your behavior and be the person you want to be.

giving yourself the gift of mindfulness

For the next week or so, do the Rest practice (chapter 1) at least once a day, preferably listening to the downloadable guided audio. Most teens find that the best times to practice are after school, before homework, between homework subjects, before bed, or before a big event like a test, a basketball game, or an audition. Do your best to create a routine that works for you. Learning mindfulness is like learning to play a sport or an instrument. The more you practice, the more skilled you'll become.

Mindfulness is ~

Paying attention, here and now, with kindness and curiosity,
so that we can choose our behavior.

part 2

beginning again

Welcome back! I'm so glad that you've chosen to return and begin this second part. Maybe you've been very consistent and practiced mindfulness every day. Maybe several weeks have gone by, and you completely forgot about the book and practicing, and then someone or something reminded you that you want to learn some skills for reducing your stress and living a happier, more fulfilling life. Either way, you're here now, ready, willing, and reading!

Sticking with a daily practice can be a lot like staying with the breath during mindfulness practice. We begin with good intentions: *I'm going to learn these skills, I'm going to practice every day, I'm going to complete this book by the end of the summer… I am going to sit down and rest my attention on my breath.* And then life happens. We get distracted, we lose track of our intentions, we forget to practice. That's normal.

What's cool is that as soon as you notice that you've forgotten, you're being mindful again. Then you can simply return: return to your intentions, to the book, to your daily practice, to the breath. There's no need for guilt, no reason to beat yourself up. Just begin again.

So take a few minutes, here and now, and rest your attention on the breath. You can listen to the guided Rest audio, or you can simply set a timer and do your best to rest your attention on the breath for five minutes.

chapter 10

Activity:
Pleasant Events

Often we are so busy, in our heads, and focused on our problems that we don't notice the pleasant events in our lives—simple moments of ease, happiness, and fun. See if you can remember a pleasant event from the last couple of days.

Social media, TV, and advertising tell us that pleasant events have to be big, exciting, and sexy, like going to a cool party, getting an amazing gift, or going on an awesome vacation. Yet pleasant events are usually brief and simple: petting your dog, laughing with a friend, solving a math problem, rocking out to your favorite song, seeing a beautiful sunset...

Once you've remembered a pleasant event, fill in the following cartoon. Just a few brief words or sketches are fine. In the thought bubble, note the thoughts that appeared during the pleasant event. In the feelings bubble, note the emotions that appeared during the event. And in the body bubble, note what was happening in your body and how your body felt during the event.

As you fill out the cartoon, it may be helpful to consider your five senses—sight, hearing, taste, touch, and smell—as well as your facial expression and body sensations.

If you're having difficulty remembering something pleasant, *think small.* Did you hear a great new song or a funny joke? As you walked to class, could you feel the sunshine or the breeze on your face? Did you share an easy moment with a friend? Did you enjoy a delicious sandwich?

Pleasant Event Cartoon

You may wonder what the point of this exercise is. Appreciating the pleasant events in our lives brings us into the present moment and is a great antidote to stress.

For survival, our minds are trained to look for problems and threats. When our distant ancestors were living in the wild, in the jungle or on the savanna, this was very helpful. However, these days, this habit makes most of us stressed because our minds mistakenly interpret ordinary daily experiences (losing your cell phone, getting a bad grade, or having an argument with a friend) as life-threatening events. When our minds do this, our bodies react and produce stress hormones, creating an almost constant low level of panic.

To balance out the mind's tendency to *negative scan*, or look for problems, and to simply enjoy our lives more, it helps to practice appreciating the pleasant moments in our lives. For the next week or so, at the end of each day before you get into bed, practice remembering a simple pleasant moment from the day. You might set up a daily reminder on your phone and use the following chart to record these events and how they affect you. Interestingly, committing to writing down a pleasant event at the end of each day often helps us notice more pleasant events throughout the day. And it lays the foundation for a more consistent gratitude practice, simply taking a few moments each day, or every week, to consider and perhaps even write down things in your life that you are grateful for. You can download additional copies of the Pleasant Events chart at http://www.newharbinger.com/33766.

Pleasant Events

What was the event?	What thoughts appeared during the event?	What feelings or emotions appeared during the event?	How did your body feel during the event?	What thoughts, feelings, and body sensations are present now, as you write about the event?
MONDAY:				
TUESDAY:				
WEDNESDAY:				

What was the event?	What thoughts appeared during the event?	What feelings or emotions appeared during the event?	How did your body feel during the event?	What thoughts, feelings, and body sensations are present now, as you write about the event?
THURSDAY:				
FRIDAY:				
SATURDAY:				
SUNDAY:				

chapter 11

Practice:
Mindful Eating

One thing that can be pleasant and that we do every day is eat. Yet often we eat so fast that we don't even taste our food. So take a moment to read the following instructions, and then give mindful eating a try.

Take a moment and, with some sense of what's actually available in your kitchen, consider what you'd like to eat. Listen to your body. What would your taste buds like? What will give you a sense of satisfaction? What will leave you feeling optimally energized rather than hyper, slow, heavy, or bloated? Even if you haven't made it to the kitchen and are still just reading, bring your kind and curious attention to what's happening in your mouth. Are you salivating? What's happening in your body? Is your stomach feeling empty or hungry? And what's happening in your mind? As you consider certain foods, do you have a sense of wanting or definitely not wanting them?

Now, if you haven't already done so, make your way to the kitchen and choose something to eat. Notice what you choose and how much you choose to serve yourself. Then commit to eating the first three bites slowly and mindfully, as described next.

Begin by looking at the food. Notice the color and the texture.

Now smell the food. How many unique flavors can you smell? What's happening in your mouth as you smell?

After you read the next few paragraphs, take one bite of the food you have chosen. Let the bite sit in your mouth for a moment without chewing. Close your eyes. Again notice what's happening in your mouth, your body, and your mind. Notice if you love the food or hate it. Notice if you really want to chew or if you want to spit it out. Go slowly. Don't rush.

When you're ready, take one chew, noticing the taste... Then continue, taking one single chew at a time, noticing how the taste changes and how your teeth and tongue work with each bite... Do your best to put all of your attention into your mouth, focusing your attention on the food, the chewing, and the tasting... Take your time... Be curious about your experience...

See if you can notice the urge to swallow before you actually swallow, and then see if you can feel the swallow as the food moves down your throat... Before you open your eyes, notice how your body, mind, and heart feel now, after eating mindfully.

Now that you have read through the instructions, you can give mindful eating a try.

chapter 12

Reflection:
How Did It Feel to Eat Mindfully?

After you've tried the Mindful Eating practice, take a few minutes to reflect on your experience, and answer the following questions.

What was it like to eat mindfully?

_____

_____

How was it different from how you usually eat?

_____

_____

What did you notice about the taste?

_____

What did you notice about the process of chewing?

_____

How did your mind feel when you put your full attention on chewing and tasting?

_____

_____

_____

Did anything about the practice surprise you? Were you surprised by how tasty one bite can be? Were you surprised that a food you thought you loved didn't actually taste that great?

_____

_____

_____

Many teens find this practice surprisingly flavorful and relaxing. They're amazed that simply slowing down and tasting their food can calm their bodies and minds. Other teens find this practice difficult and annoying. They find that they dislike the taste or the texture of the food. They think the practice is too slow and feel impatient. Whether you found the practice peaceful or annoying, delicious or disgusting, as long as you gave your kind and curious attention to your experience, you practiced mindfulness. Again, being mindful doesn't mean being blissed out; it means being fully aware of your experience in the moment.

giving yourself the gift of mindfulness

I encourage you to practice mindfulness for a few minutes every day. Mindfulness is a learnable skill, like shooting free throws or rehearsing a piece of music. Usually when we are first learning something new, we feel a bit awkward and unsure. Over time, with practice, we become more skillful; the basics feel more solid and reliable. And when we have developed a certain level of mastery, we can be creative and begin to improvise in new situations. It is the same with mindfulness. At first the practice may feel unusual and clumsy. But most teens find that with just a few minutes of daily practice, their mindfulness muscles get stronger and more flexible, and they find that using mindfulness makes their everyday lives less stressful and more enjoyable. But don't take my word for it. Do your best to practice every day, and see what happens for you.

Over the next week or so, commit to practicing mindfulness and self-care:

* Do the Rest practice (from chapter 1) once a day.

* Eat one bite or, better yet, one snack mindfully every day.

* Notice pleasant events, and chart one at the end of each day.

Mindfulness is ~

Simple. Just this moment. Here. Now.

part 3

thought watching
and unkind mind

As you've been reading this book, there have been several times when I've invited you to become aware of your thoughts. Being aware of thoughts is a powerful tool; ultimately it allows us to live our lives as we choose rather than being controlled by our thoughts. Our thoughts are often inaccurate, unkind, and dramatic. Maybe you know people who like to gossip and stir things up. Perhaps you have learned to not take these people too seriously, to check out what they say and find out if it is true before acting on what they've told you. Our minds are often like gossips, and so it's wise not to take them too seriously. The next few chapters will help you practice—watching thoughts, noticing patterns, questioning their accuracy, opening to other possiblities, and then choosing how to respond. Don't worry if this sounds confusing; it will become clear. Let's begin.

chapter 13

Practice:
Thought Watching

This practice will support you in bringing your kind and curious attention to the process of thinking. As with the Rest practice (in chapter 1), the easiest way to do this is to download the audio version from http://www.newharbinger.com/33766. Alternatively you can read through the following instructions and then set a timer for five minutes and practice watching thoughts come and go.

Start by sitting or lying in a comfortable position with your back straight, your body relaxed, and your eyes closed. Bring your attention to the breath and to the rhythmic expansion and release of the breath in the belly. Use the breath to settle into the Still Quiet Place between the in-breath and the out-breath…

Remember that if you find yourself lost in thought, you can return to the Still Quiet Place at any time simply by refocusing your attention on the rhythm of the breath…

Now begin watching your thoughts, as though you were standing on a sidewalk watching people walk by… Perhaps you can notice when a particular thought comes into view, passes by, and then moves out of sight.

Perhaps you can notice that thoughts, like people, have personalities. Some are loud, others are shy, some are funny, others are somewhat cruel, and some are stubborn, coming back again and again…and again.

Just sitting, breathing, and watching the thoughts.

Do your best to stay on the sidewalk and let the thoughts go by rather than walk down the street with them.

And when you find yourself walking with the thoughts (which we all do), congratulate yourself for noticing. Then return your attention to the breath, feeling the rhythm of the in-breath and the out-breath… When your attention is stable, you can begin again, to watch the thoughts.

You may notice that some thoughts are alone while others travel in groups, or that one thought can gather a crowd of thoughts, feelings, and physical experiences, like a headache or a smile…

Just keep breathing and watching…

With practice, you may find moments when the thoughts drift into the background…

What is it that has the power to watch the thoughts?

It is your Still Quiet Place, or another word for it is awareness. See if you can rest in awareness and let the thoughts walk by.

Stay here watching your thoughts for as long as you like. And remember, you can always choose to rest in the Still Quiet Place and watch the thoughts go by, without believing them or taking them personally.

So now that you have read the practice, set your timer and give thought watching a try.

chapter 14

Reflection: How Did It Feel to Watch Your Thoughts?

Now that you have watched your thoughts for a few minutes, consider the following questions. Do your best not to overthink. There are no right or wrong answers. Just jot down what is true for you.

Were you able, at least some of the time, to watch thoughts come and go?

Circle one: Yes.   No.   Sort of.

If you were able to watch thoughts come and go, that's great. If not, trust that it will come with practice. Keep using your kind and curious attention to discover that thoughts come and go, just like the breath comes and goes during Rest practice (chapter 1) and sounds come and go in Listening practice (chapter 7).

When you reflect on the thoughts you noticed during the practice, what percentage of the thoughts would you estimate were about

The future, such as your plans for the evening or a test coming up? _____

The past, such as an argument you had with your mom or a pleasant memory? _____

The present, this moment, here and now? _____

What percentage of the thoughts were generally

Kind? _____

Unkind? _____

Neutral? _____

What percentage of your thoughts would you say were true? _____ (Note: it is extremely unlikely that 100 percent of the thoughts are true.)

Did you notice any patterns to your thinking? If so, describe them here:

_____

_____

_____

When you got lost in thinking, walking down the street with the thoughts instead of watching them walk past, how often were you eventually able to notice, return your attention to the breath, and begin again?

Circle one:　　　Rarely.　　Sometimes.　　Often.

Were you lost in thinking, walking down the street with your thoughts, when the timer went off?

Circle one:　　　Yes.　　No.　　Sort of.

chapter 15

Basic Concept:
Head in the Game

Thought watching can be tricky. You may wonder if it's worth the effort. You may wonder exactly how it can help you. If so, you aren't alone. One morning, I was guiding some students through the thought-watching practice. It was a class where most of the boys had been quite skeptical of mindfulness. Some of the boys were on the basketball team, and that morning they noticed that almost all of their thoughts were about the game they'd be playing that afternoon. They'd lost the previous game, and now they were up against a team they *thought* was better than they were. Many of them had thoughts or worries about losing, playing poorly, and letting their teammates down. All of them had thoughts about wanting to win.

During our previous sessions, a boy I'll call Jonathan had made it clear that he had doubts about this whole mindfulness thing. (By the way, doubts are absolutely fine, and I encourage you to not take my word about the benefits of mindfulness. Rather, give it an honest try, do the practices in the book, and decide for yourself if you find it useful.) Anyway, after Jonathan had shared his thoughts, I asked him, "If you're thinking about winning and losing, and how good the other team is, and letting your teammates down, is your head *really* in the game? Is it really in what's happening right here, right now?" His eyes got big. His mouth opened. He had that "aha" look. He got it! He understood that if, while playing, he was busy thinking about winning and losing, or about how good the other team is, or about letting his teammates down, he wasn't actually *playing* the game 100 percent.

It helped to be able to tell the class that two of the most successful teams ever in the history of professional basketball, the Los Angeles Lakers and the Chicago Bulls, used mindfulness skills to bring their full attention to actually *playing* the game—to the ball, the hoop, their teammates, and their opponents. In fact, many successful athletes and teams use mindfulness to improve their performance, including the USA BMX cycling team, three-time beach volleyball Olympic gold medalists Kerri Walsh Jennings and Misty May-Treanor, the San Francisco Giants' World Series pitcher Tim Lincecum, US national soccer team member Clint Dempsey, 2006 Olympic silver medalist and three-time world champion figure skater Sasha Cohen, and recent Super Bowl champions the Seattle Seahawks. One of my greatest joys as an athlete and a person who practices mindfulness is helping athletes learn mindfulness.

The next exercise will help you become aware of the thoughts that appear when you face a new challenge; being aware of your thoughts will help you face daily challenges like these elite athletes do.

chapter 16

Activity:
Nine Dots

Now that you have the basic idea of thought watching, you can apply this skill to working on a puzzle. First take a moment to breathe and rest in stillness and quietness.

When you're ready, give yourself five minutes to try to solve this puzzle. As you're trying to solve the puzzle, notice the thoughts that come and go, and notice how you talk to yourself.

Nine Dots Puzzle

Below is an arrangement of nine dots. Connect all the dots by drawing four straight lines without lifting your pencil from the paper, and without retracing any line. The lines may cross.

●　　　　　●　　　　　●

●　　　　　●　　　　　●

●　　　　　●　　　　　●

Before you look at the answer (in the appendix) take some time to write about your experience. What did you say to yourself as you tried to solve the puzzle? There is no good or bad, right or wrong, here. Just be real with yourself. What did you honestly think?

_____

_____

_____

_____

_____

_____

_____

_____

_____

_____

_____

_____

_____

_____

_____

Here are some things that other teens have said out loud, or silently to themselves, while trying to solve this puzzle. They have said, "Puzzles are dumb." "I can't get this." "I'll figure it out." "I am bad at math and puzzles." "I got it!" "I'll just Google it." "I love these kinds of games." "I'm stupid." "I give up."

Now that you know what other teens have said, is there anything you might add to what you wrote before? Remember what it was like to try doing the puzzle, and then take a moment to write down three more things you said to yourself. Again, there's no right or wrong here. And it is very helpful to be aware of your patterns and habits of thinking.

_____

_____

_____

_____

Do you often say similar things to yourself when facing other challenges, such as doing a difficult homework assignment or learning a new athletic skill or a musical piece?

Circle one: Yes.   No.   Sometimes.

Was what you said to yourself mostly kind or unkind?   _____

Was it mostly helpful or discouraging?   _____

Do you feel it was mostly true or untrue?   _____

When you try something new and challenging, what are you generally tempted to do?

Circle one: Quit.   Keep trying.   Cheat.   Ask for help.   Other: _____

What could you have said to yourself that would have been more kind and helpful?

_____

_____

_____

If you solved the puzzle, notice the thoughts and feelings that come with this experience. If you haven't solved the puzzle, here are a couple of hints: there are actually four solutions, one starting in each corner, and all of the solutions involve thinking outside the box. Give yourself another five minutes to play with the puzzle. See if you can be kind and encouraging with yourself. If you've already given up or are unable to encourage yourself, do your best to bring kindness and curiosity to the experience of giving up, just as it is, in this moment.

Kindness and curiosity are *always* an option, even when, or *especially* when, we're being hard on ourselves or we've given up. If that feels hard to believe and to do, don't worry. It will become easier as you continue reading this book and practicing mindfulness.

Okay, enough! The answer is in the appendix, and before you turn to look, please know that this exercise isn't about getting the "right" answer. It's about bringing your kind and curious attention (yes, this phrase will be repeated over and over, until it's lodged in your head and your heart) to your life. So when you see the solution to the puzzle, do your best to notice your thoughts and feelings with kindness and curiosity.

chapter 17

Activity:
Thinking Outside the Box

The solutions to the Nine Dots Puzzle required noticing and then thinking outside the box. With kindness and curiosity, consider some of the boxes—categories you put yourself and others into—that affect your life.

What kinds of boxes do you put yourself in? Some common boxes are thoughts like *I'm not a science person, I'm a talented musician, I'm depressed, I suck at sports, I'm popular, I'm not popular, I'm a good student,* or *I'm a bad student.*

Write down three boxes that describe how you think of yourself.

_____

_____

_____

Now consider whether these boxes feel helpful, true, big enough…

Are any of the boxes a source of stress?

Circle one: Yes.   No.   Sort of.

Many of the boxes we put ourselves in can create stress. It is easy to see how negative or unkind boxes, like *I'm ugly*, create stress. It can be more difficult to see how the positive boxes create stress, and they definitely can. Say one of your boxes is *I'm kind*, or *I'm great at creative writing*. What happens when you are unkind or you write a story that's only okay?

Boxes can be helpful and serve a function, and they never tell the whole story. If I know that I have dyslexia, which I do, and I put myself in the dyslexic box, then I can get help with my reading, writing, and editing. And my dyslexia is not who I am; it doesn't define me. We are all so much more than any of our boxes. So it is helpful to be aware of our boxes and not let them define us.

chapter 18

Activity:
Boxes and Others

We aren't the only ones putting us in boxes. Take a moment and, with kindness and curiosity—and even a sense of humor—consider the boxes that others put you in. List three boxes for each category.

Boxes your parents or adults in your family put you in:

1. _____

2. _____

3. _____

Boxes your siblings put you in:

1. _____

2. _____

3. _____

Boxes your teachers put you in:

1. _____

2. _____

3. _____

Boxes your friends put you in:

1. _____

2. _____

3. _____

Consider the pluses and minuses of each box. For example, it can be really great to be in the "He's so funny" box, and it can also be kind of exhausting and tough if you want to be taken seriously, or if you're feeling down and could use some support.

Most importantly, always remember this: *You are so much more than the boxes you or anyone else puts you in.*

Now take a moment and bring a good friend into your mind and heart. List three boxes you put this person in:

1. _____

2. _____

3. _____

Perhaps one box you put your friend in is "kind person." Can you see that the boxes don't capture everything about your friend, and that your friend, like all human beings, can have unkind moments?

Now pause, take three slow, deep breaths and choose to bring kind and curious attention to a more challenging person, someone you're having difficulty with. Bring that difficult person into your mind and heart. Yup, that person. The first person who came to mind. Now list three boxes you put him or her in.

1. _____

2. _____

3. _____

Can you see that these boxes don't capture everything about this challenging person, any more than your boxes—the ones that you (and others) put you in—capture everything about you?

When I become aware that I've put myself or someone else in a box, I like to challenge myself to find at least *one* moment when the person acts outside the box. For example, sometimes my husband is my difficult person and I put him in the "impatient" box. When this happens, and I remember, I find it very helpful to actively work on noticing when he *is* patient.

So take another moment to bring your kind and curious attention to this person whom you find so difficult, and consider what might cause him or her to act in the ways that annoy you. If you're unable or unwilling to consider this, and think, *He's just a jerk*, then notice this thought with kindness and curiosity. Still, maybe a crabby teacher has a sick child or a dying parent. Maybe that mean or rude girl's parents are getting divorced, or maybe she's actually really insecure.

Don't get me wrong. I'm not excusing unkind behavior or suggesting that you hang out or put up with someone who is mean or rude. And it is helpful to understand that unkind and even cruel behavior—mine, yours, or that of people we find difficult—comes out of pain.

Just like you want to be seen for your whole amazing self, this difficult person wants to be seen as his or her whole amazing self. How might these people act if seen in their wholeness as flawed and amazing human beings? How might the world be different if everyone were seen in their wholeness as the flawed *and* amazing human beings they are?

Remember that others are so much more than the boxes we put them in.

chapter 19

Basic Concept:
If You Spot It, You Got It

It is a natural human tendency to put others in boxes. And as you are learning, boxes don't capture the whole person. One fun way to play with this is the very brief practice of "If you spot it, you got it," also known as "One finger pointing out, three fingers pointing back." Let's try this, and then I'll explain it a bit more.

Think about the boxes that you put your good friend in (return to the list in chapter 18). For each of the boxes that you listed for your friend, you can discover where you have the same quality. Now there may be some *skills* that your friend has—like being a great musician—that you don't have, but with qualities like kindness or a sense of humor, if you can recognize them in your friend, then you have them in yourself, at least to some extent.

Okay, now let's move on to the more challenging part of this practice. Take a look at your list for the challenging person. For each of the boxes you listed for this person, can you discover where you have the same quality? I know from personal experience that this can be very uncomfortable. And if I am *really* honest, I can always find where I have the same qualities that I find challenging in someone else. As I mentioned before, I sometimes put my husband in the impatient box, and when I pause and look carefully, I realize that I am often impatient with his impatience!

This is a tricky one. So I encourage you to be extremely brave and real. Just experiment with it, and see what you discover. For me, when I recognize that despite my best intentions, I can sometimes be mean, judgmental, and arrogant, especially if I am feeling tired, upset, or insecure, then I can often be more understanding with others when they are behaving in these ways.

chapter 20

Activity:
Facing Challenges

As you've seen, one valuable lesson from doing the Nine Dots Puzzle is that it's worthwhile to look outside the box—including the boxes we put ourselves and others in. Doing this puzzle is also useful for exploring how we face challenges.

As part of the activity, you considered whether what you were saying to yourself was kind or unkind and whether it was helpful or discouraging (see chapter 16). Now, in this moment of relative calm, list three specific, helpful actions that you can take the next time you face a challenge. Perhaps listing three actions feels like a challenge, so here's a hint—take your time, be patient, and notice what comes to mind.

1. _____

2. _____

3. _____

When you're ready, whether you've listed your three actions or you feel stuck, you can look on the next page for some suggestions.

Get a snack.

Get some exercise

Ask a friend, teacher, or mentor for help.

Take a shower.

Review any instructions you have.

Choose to give up.

SLEEP ON IT.

Encourage yourself.

Listen to music.

Try again.

Take a Break.

chapter 21

Activity:
Unkind Mind

During the Nine Dots activity, I asked you to consider whether the thoughts that you were having about yourself and about the puzzle were kind or unkind (see chapter 16). Take a moment now to remember what thoughts appeared as you worked on the puzzle…

Now do your best to estimate the percentage of thoughts that were

Kind and helpful: _____

Unkind and discouraging: _____

If you're like most people, your percentages skew toward unkind and discouraging. I have a nickname for that type of inner mental chatter: Unkind Mind. This type of thinking, which can be very repetitive, is judgmental, bossy, and crabby. Unkind Mind says things like *I can't do this, I'm stupid, Math is stupid,* or *I'm going to fail.* This voice also tends to make things seem worse than they are by exaggerating, being dramatic, and distorting the truth—saying things like *This is impossible, I'm hideously ugly, Everybody hates me,* or *I am the dumbest kid in the class.* Unkind Mind also often judges other people or situations with statements like *He's a jerk* or *History is dumb.*

List three things Unkind Mind frequently says about you:

1. _____

2. _____

3. _____

List three things Unkind Mind frequently says about others, school, or life:

1. _____

2. _____

3. _____

Now, here's the most important thing to know about Unkind Mind: *You don't need to believe Unkind Mind or take what it says personally.* Practice seeing where Unkind Mind lies, gossips, or exaggerates.

chapter 22

Basic Concept:
Getting Real

We are often unaware of what we're thinking and feeling. And even if we're aware of what we're thinking and feeling, we sometimes pretend that we aren't, because we feel bad, embarrassed, or ashamed about our thoughts and feelings. It's helpful to remember that everybody has thoughts and feelings, that thoughts and feelings come and go, and that most of our thoughts and feelings aren't unique.

One Friday morning as I was guiding a class of tenth graders through Thought Watching practice (see chapter 13), two girls chose to chat and file their nails. As I led the practice, I meandered down the aisle and eventually stood by their desks. Continuing to lead the practice, I simply said, "Notice your thoughts. For example, you may be thinking about your homework or your plans for the weekend, or you may be thinking *Why the F is she standing by my desk?*" They stopped talking.

After the practice, the more courageous of the two asked somewhat suspiciously, "Can you read minds?" I said, "No, I can't read minds. But I *have* a mind, and my mind is very much like your mind. I've spent a lot of time watching my mind, so I have a pretty good idea of what your mind might say." By being *completely* real about what I would have thought if I were her, I helped her be aware of her thoughts and understand that they were very ordinary. This increased her curiosity about mindfulness and also increased her willingness to practice.

I am sharing this example with you so that you realize that we *all* have these types of thoughts—*F you, He is such an a-hole, I just want to deck him, I can't live like this, I give up*—and that with practice, we can learn to watch these thoughts and then *choose* whether we act on them or not.

giving yourself the gift of mindfulness

For the next week or so, I encourage you to bring kind and curious attention to the process of thinking, to notice patterns and habits of thinking, including whether your thoughts are true, kind, and helpful. It is enough to simply rest in stillness and quietness and observe your thoughts; there is no need to change them, fix them, or make them go away. When we rest in stillness and quietness and observe our thoughts, we are less caught up in them, and we can see ourselves, others, and events in our lives more clearly. Experiment with these practices for the next week or so and see what you discover:

* Practice with the Thought Watching audio once a day (see chapter 13).

* Bring kindness and curiosity to your thinking, including—especially!— thoughts that put you, others, or situations in very tight boxes.

* Notice when Unkind Mind shows up. What does it say?

* Remember, you can choose whether to believe your thoughts and Unkind Mind.

Mindfulness is ~

Curious: a way of exploring both your inner world and the outer world.

part 4

feelings and unpleasant events

In part 3, you practiced bringing your kind and curious attention to your thinking. Now you will learn to bring the same kind and curious attention to physical sensations and feelings. The Finger Yoga activity will help you notice physical sensations in your body, and the Befriending Feelings practice will support you in gently opening to the emotions we all experience. As you practice, you'll realize that physical sensations and emotions come and go, just like thoughts, sounds, and the breath. In time, even the most intense, awful emotions will pass. This is especially important to know and remember when you're feeling very upset or depressed.

chapter 23

Activity:
Finger Yoga

Place your left hand on your left thigh. *Gently* use your right index and middle finger to pull the fourth finger on your left hand backward. Notice your limit—the place where you need to stop pulling to avoid causing pain or injury.

The purpose of this very simple exercise is for you to practice really listening to your body, stretching gently to your current limit, and backing off a bit when things get too intense.

Now perhaps you can consider doing some other simple stretches. For example, you can stand and stretch both arms up overhead and then lean from your waist in an arc to the right, creating a C shape with your body and feeling the sensations of the stretch… Then repeat the stretch to the other side, leaning to the left… As you stretch, keep breathing naturally and bring your kind and curious attention to the experience of stretching.

For another stretch, stand and clasp your hands together behind your back. Then gently raise your arms up behind you as high as you can while keeping your chest up, feeling the sensations in your chest, shoulders, and arms. Play with stretching just a bit beyond your comfort zone. Notice how your body, mind, and heart feel after doing these simple stretches. (A downloadable stretching and balancing practice can be found at http://www.newharbinger.com/33766.)

With practice, you can learn to gently stretch into discomfort not only in your body but also in other areas of your life. For example, if you have a challenging school assignment or an emotional upset, you can experiment with stretching and easing into your frustration or sadness. Maybe you can try just being with your frustration or sadness for three full breaths.

We will explore this more in the next chapter. For now it may be helpful to know that you can gently stretch into physical, mental, and emotional experiences that are uncomfortable. And just like when you stretch your body, when you stretch your mind and heart, they become stronger, more flexible, and more balanced. And, as with physical stretching, when you are stretching in other areas of your life, it is important to know when to stop stretching, to release, to ask for help.

chapter 24

Practice:
Befriending Feelings

This practice involves bringing kind and curious attention to your feelings, or emotions. (A downloadable version of this practice is available at http://www .newharbinger.com/33766.)

As usual, sit or lie in a comfortable position…find the breath in your belly…and rest in stillness and quietness… When you are ready, simply note whatever feelings are present. Sometimes it can be helpful to name each feeling. Some feelings may have ordinary names—like *angry, happy, sad,* or *excited*—and others may have more unusual names, like *stormy, bubbly, fiery,* or *empty.* It can be helpful to know that feelings may be small or subtle and kind of shy, or big and intense, that feelings may shift over time, and that there may be layers of feelings.

Once you've brought your kind and curious attention to a particular feeling and you've named it, notice where the feeling lives in your body: sitting in your chest, stirring in your belly, resting in your big toe… Also notice *how* this emotion *feels* in your body. Does it feel small or big…heavy or light…soft or hard…warm or cool…? Is it moving or still…?

If any of these questions shift you into *thinking* about feelings rather than *experiencing* them, simply breathe and return to *being* with the feelings as they come and go.

Next, notice whether the feeling has a color, or colors, or imagine that it does—perhaps dark red, pale blue, or bright green… And if it doesn't have a color, that is fine.

And listen to see whether the feeling has a sound, such as giggling, groaning, or whining… And if it doesn't have a sound, no worries.

Now, kindly ask the feeling what it wants from you. Usually feelings want something simple, like acceptance, time, space, or a way to express themselves. Are you willing and able to give the feeling what it asked for? If not, no problem. Sometimes feelings want things from us that we can't or don't want to give, or that it would be unwise to give. We'll address this more in coming chapters.

To end the practice, notice how you feel now, and congratulate yourself for taking the time to be with and befriend your feelings. Then rest briefly, again, in stillness and quietness.

chapter 25

Reflection:
How Did It Feel to
Befriend Your Feelings?

Take some time now to reflect on your experience with the Befriending Feelings
practice in chapter 24. Here are some questions to guide your reflection.

What feeling or feelings were present?

_____

_____

Where did you *feel* these emotions in your body?

_____

_____

How did the emotions *feel* (soft or hard, warm or cool...)?

_____

_____

Did the emotions have colors?

_____

_____

Did they have any sounds?

_____

_____

What did the emotions want from you?

_____

_____

Were you able to give the feelings what they wanted?

Circle one: Yes.   No.   Sort of.   (Again, if the answer is no, that's fine.)

chapter 26

Basic Concept:
Befriending Feelings

Just like our real friends, sometimes feelings want something that we're unwilling or unable to give. Or they may want something that it wouldn't be wise for us to give. For example, greed may want us to steal something, despair may want us to cut ourselves, or anger may want us to punch someone. In these situations, it can be helpful to talk with the feelings, just like you would talk to a friend.

That may sound a little weird, so here's an example of such a discussion, provided by my daughter, Nicole. She's a teenager now and has kindly given me permission to share a very simple conversation she had with fear when she was in fourth grade. To set the stage, it was the evening before her school talent show. That afternoon's rehearsal hadn't gone well. She had "messed up." She felt afraid that she would mess up again in the actual talent show in front of "the whole school." When I guided her through the Befriending Feelings practice you just learned, and she asked the fear what it wanted from her, her fear said it wanted to be in charge.

Although this story isn't about me, I will say that my initial thoughts at the time were *Wait, fear can't want that... That's not how the practice goes. A feeling is supposed to want time, space, and attention...* However, I took fear at its word and asked Nicole, "How do you feel about that?"

She said, "I don't want it to be in charge."

I said, "Okay, so tell it that."

She told it that, and fear said, "Well, I still want to be in charge." A few moments later, Nicole told her fear, "You can come, but you can't be in charge." Fear agreed to this compromise. Nicole chose to symbolize the agreement by putting a small Guatemalan worry doll in the pocket of her dress. So fear got to go, and joy was in charge. The next chapter has some suggestions for how to work with more typical teenage issues, especially when intense feelings want you to do something unwise or unhealthy.

chapter 27

Activity:
Befriending Feelings

Now the fourth grade example in the last chapter may seem simple and silly compared to some of the things you are dealing with as a teenager. But when you have intense feelings that are asking you to do something unwise or unhealthy, it can be helpful to take a few minutes to have a conversation with those feelings and write down both sides of the discussion. Kick it around, hash it out, just like you would with a friend who's proposing something that you *know* in your heart is a *bad idea.*

Here are some helpful questions to ask and some helpful statements to use when speaking with these kinds of feelings:

Questions:

What do you think that will get us?

How do you think we'll feel after we do that?

What will the consequences be in the outer world, like with my parents, teachers, friends, school, or the police?

What will the consequences be in my inner world? Will I feel good about myself? Will I feel guilty? Proud? Ashamed?

Statements:

I am not willing to do that.

I know that ultimately that behavior will make me feel worse because…

I know that ultimately that behavior will cause problems because…

I am willing to…

Here are some examples of what you might tell different feelings you're willing to do:

To greed, you might say, *I am willing to…*

> *…do odd jobs and save money to buy that.*

> *…buy something that's similar and less expensive.*

> *…appreciate what I do have.*

To sadness, you might say, *I am willing to…*

> *…express you in writing or drawing.*

> *…talk to a friend or counselor.*

> *…be with you for ten slow, deep breaths.*

To anger, you might say, *I am willing to…*

> *…go for a run.*

> *…wait until I'm clear and can express you in words rather than violence.*

> *…crush some cans with a baseball bat.*

> *…be with you for ten slow, deep breaths.*

Note: Usually the process of dialoguing with feelings brings clarity and ease. However, if as you dialogue the feeling becomes intense, demanding, or obsessive, simply return to just *being* with the feeling. And if needed, seek support from a trusted adult.

Here is a place for you to write out your dialogue with the feelings.

You: *Hello feeling(s). What do you want from me?*

_____

Feeling(s): *I (we) want...* _____

_____

You: _____

_____

Feeling(s): _____

_____

You: _____

_____

Feeling(s): _____

_____

You: _____

_____

Feeling(s): _____

_____

You: _____

_____

Feeling(s): _____

_____

You: _____

_____

Feeling(s): _____

_____

You: _____

_____

Feeling(s): _____

_____

You: _____

_____

Feeling(s): _____

_____

chapter 28

Activity:
Expressing Feelings

I've shared the Befriending Feelings practice (in chapter 24) with lots of teens, in schools, in the community, and in my office, and many of them like to express their feelings through singing or rapping, drawing, creating abstract art or intricate grafitti, or writing haikus or cartoons. In this activity, I invite you to play with creatively expressing your feelings.

If you choose to write a haiku, you don't need to make it fit the strict format of five syllables in the first line, seven syllables in the second line, and five syllables in the last line. For now, we will define a *feelings haiku* as a statement or poem that can be said in one breath.

Even if you usually *think* that drawing and writing are not your thing, you may find these simple ways of expressing feelings helpful. They are certainly more useful than some of our unhealthy habits for dealing with feelings: pretending we are fine; stuffing our feelings; numbing out; acting out; overeating; bingeing on TV, video games, or social media; drinking…the list goes on. In fact, many of our usual strategies often end up making us feel worse in the long run. So in the space on the next page, give writing or drawing a try.

If you really get into this, or if you want to express yourself through music or other art forms, you may need an entirely different format from the simple blank space here. Whatever works for you is great! The key is to find a way to acknowledge and express your feelings. Put on a song that matches your feelings, throw rocks at a metal garbage can, go outside and scream, stand in the shower and cry, have a dance party in your room…

chapter 29

Activity:
Having Your Feelings Without Your Feelings Having You

You've been practicing watching, befriending, and expressing your feelings. There is real power in learning to have your feelings without your feelings having you. What does this mean? "Having your feelings" means being aware of what you're feeling in the moment. "Without your feelings having you" means your feelings don't have control over your behavior or make you do or say something that you might regret.

Can you think of a time in the recent past where your feelings had you? Describe the situation, what happened, how you felt, and what you did because of the feeling:

_____

_____

_____

Looking back now, what might you have done differently?

_____

_____

_____

chapter 30

Basic Concept:
Dealing with Feelings

It can be helpful to understand that each of us tends to have habits, certain ways we usually deal with our feelings. Without mindfulness, most of us tend to live within a fairly narrow range along the continuum from ignoring (suppressing) feelings to being overwhelmed (controlled) by them. Take a moment and consider what you tend to do with intense feelings.

←——————————————————————————————→

Ignoring feelings   **Being overwhelmed by feelings**

For those of us who usually ignore and suppress our feelings, the Befriending Feelings practice (in chapter 24) can support us in bringing kindness and curiosity to our emotions, making us more emotionally intelligent. For those of us who tend to be flooded and overwhelmed by our feelings, it can be helpful to take some time to *really* settle into the Still Quiet Place *before* we do the Befriending Feelings practice. With practice, we can all learn to have our feelings (most of the time) without our feelings having us. Ultimately, this allows us to live our lives in ways we feel good about.

chapter 31

Basic Concept:
Emotions Beneath Boredom

Many teens frequently say they feel bored. First, I would like to suggest that "I feel bored" is a thought rather than a feeling. And if you repeatedly think you are bored, I invite you to look underneath the boredom. Often, you may discover sadness, anger, or fear. For example, a young man in one of my courses, whom I will call Alan, repeatedly reported that he was bored, so I checked in with him after class one day. To make a long story short, it turned out that Alan had chosen not to share either on his intake form or during class that his father had recently had an affair and abruptly moved out of the country to be with his new girlfriend. I appreciated that Alan was brave and trusted me enough to share this difficult situation. This new information gave me a fresh view of Alan's circumstances. It prompted me to suggest that he look underneath his boredom to see if perhaps there were other feelings he might not be acknowledging. Not surprisingly, he discovered anger, sadness, and confusion. Over time with practice, Alan was able to acknowledge and express his complex, multilayered feelings about his father's betrayal and departure.

chapter 32

Activity:
Unpleasant Events

In chapter 10, you brought kind and curious attention to your experience of pleasant events. You can do the same with unpleasant events. Take a moment to remember an unpleasant event from the last few days. It doesn't need to be a big deal, although it can be. When you have an event in mind, fill in the following cartoon.

Just a few brief words or sketches are fine. In the thought bubble, note the thoughts that appeared during the unpleasant event. In the feelings bubble, note the emotions that appeared during the event. And in the body bubble, note what was happening in your body and how your body *felt* during the event.

Remember, as you fill out the page it may be helpful to consider your five senses—sight, hearing, taste, touch, and smell—as well as your facial expression and physical sensations.

Unpleasant Event Cartoon

Now, just as you did for pleasant events, for the next week or so, bring your kind and curious attention to unpleasant events. At the end of each day, use the following chart to record these events and how they affect you. You might want to be especially curious about whether there are any themes or patterns to the events and your inner experience.

Unpleasant Events

What was the event?	What thoughts appeared during the event?	What feelings or emotions appeared during the event?	How did your body feel during the event?	What thoughts, feelings, and body sensations are present now, as you write about the event?
MONDAY:				
TUESDAY:				
WEDNESDAY:				

What was the event?	What thoughts appeared during the event?	What feelings or emotions appeared during the event?	How did your body feel during the event?	What thoughts, feelings, and body sensations are present now, as you write about the event?
THURSDAY:				
FRIDAY:				
SATURDAY:				
SUNDAY:				

chapter 33

Basic Concept:
Suffering = Pain x Resistance

Here's something you may have already discovered for yourself: much of the suffering related to an unpleasant event often has to do with our thoughts and feelings about the event. And much of that thinking and feeling has to do with the past or, more often, the future: *My dad won't let me hang out with my friends today* becomes *My dad never lets me hang out with my friends.* And *I'm bored now* expands into *I'm going to be bored forever.* And *I can't solve this physics problem* turns into *I'm stupid, and I won't be able to solve any of the problems, ever.* The essence of most of this upsetting thinking and feeling is resistance; resistance is basically wanting things to be different.

My friend and colleague Gina Biegel, who's done scientific research documenting the benefits of teaching mindfulness to teens, shares the following mathematical equation from Shinzen Young:

Suffering = Pain x Resistance

If these words are confusing, you can think of *suffering* as being upset, *pain* as unpleasantness, and *resistance* as wanting things to be different. In other words, when something unpleasant happens, how upset you feel is the product of the unpleasantness multiplied by how much you want things to be different.

Often, though not always, the level of pain (or unpleasantness) is fixed and cannot be changed, and the only part of the equation we can adjust is our resistance (how much we want things to be different).

Let's make this more real with an example. Say that, for you, not making the soccer team or not getting a role in a play is a 7 on a pain scale from 1 to 10 (with 1 being very little pain and 10 being extreme pain). Resisting the outcome with thoughts like *The selection process was unfair* might be a 7 on a similar scale of resistance. So in this scenario, your level of suffering is 49. That's how upset you are. An example of a different way of thinking that might have a lower resistance score is *I am really disappointed, and I'm going to work hard and try again.* Perhaps, this type of thinking would have a resistance score of 3. This thinking doesn't change the pain of not making the team or getting a role in the play, but it does decrease the intensity of your suffering from 49 to 21. And an added bonus is that this type of thinking gives you a way to move forward—a wise next step, a specific action to take.

If that example seems a little abstract, consider the next dialogue, which I had with Maria and her classmates during a mindfulness course for high school students. This dialogue combines the Unpleasant Events activity (from chapter 32) with the concept of Suffering = Pain x Resistance. It involves an unpleasant event that most of us resist: doing homework (remember my bookkeeping).

Me: So Maria, what was your unpleasant experience?

Maria: Doing my math homework.

Me: And on a scale of one to ten, how unpleasant was it?

Maria: An eleven.

Group: Yeah, at least eleven.

Me: Okay, it may be an eleven. I'll take your word for it. And I'm going to invite you to consider if it really is an eleven. For me, an eleven would be my child getting in a serious accident, my house burning down, or someone I love dying.

Maria: Okay, probably not an eleven. Maybe a seven.

Me: Okay, seven. Now, what were your thoughts about your homework and your ability to do it?

Maria: My thoughts were "I hate this stupid homework. And I can't do it."

Group: Yeah!

Maria: "…And I can't do it. I'm stupid. I give up."

Me: And what were your feelings?

Maria: Mad, stupid, hopeless.

Me: And what was happening in your body?

Maria: I had a headache, and I felt stressed.

Me: And how does stress feel in your body?

Maria: Like tightness.

Me: And taken all together—your thoughts, your feelings, your headache, and tightness—on a scale of one to ten, how much resistance did you have?

Maria: Eight.

Me: So what was your suffering score?

Maria: Seven times eight, that's…fifty-six?

Me: Yup. Now, assuming that you can't change your homework and make it magically disappear or make it do itself, how might you decrease your suffering?

Maria: By decreasing my resistance?

Me: And how might you do that?

Maria: By not calling it "stupid" and by looking back at my notes?

Me: That sounds like a great start! When you say that, how does it feel in your body?

Maria: Less tight, better, relaxed.

Me: So how about if all of you who've had homework as an unpleasant event experiment with decreasing your resistance this week, and report back?

Many teens find the Suffering = Pain x Resistance equation to be really helpful when dealing with upsetting situations. As you read this book, you may be working with a profoundly painful situation, such as your parents getting divorced, your family dealing with financial hardship, or the loss of a friend or someone else close to you. In these cases, to honor your experience, you may increase the pain scale. For me, having my brother go to jail would be an 11 on a scale of 1 to 10. If you're dealing with an extremely painful situation, take a moment in stillness and tenderly acknowledge that pain... Go easy... Be gentle...

If your pain score is higher than 10, I encourage you to seek support from a friend, school counselor, therapist, religious leader, or doctor.

It is also important to be clear on two points:

Wanting things to be different isn't bad or wrong; it's very natural.

Acknowledging things the way they are doesn't necessarily mean giving up and not doing anything to change the situation.

Remember that wanting things to be different than they actually are usually increases suffering or upset. And usually, acknowledging things as they are, no matter how terrible, helps us make good (wise) choices about what to do next, such as go over your math notes, talk to the soccer coach or theater director to get feedback, or seek out support for yourself or a family member.

chapter 34

Activity:
Calculating Your Suffering

Using one of your examples from the What Stresses You Out? activity (in chapter 3) or a new example, calculate your suffering score for a painful or unpleasant event in your life. Again, you can use the equation

$$Suffering = Pain \times Resistance$$

Use a scale of 1 to 10 for both pain (unpleasantness) and resistance (wanting things to be different). For pain, 1 means not very painful or upsetting, and 10 means extremely upsetting. For resistance, 1 means you'd prefer something to be different, and 10 means you don't want to live with things the way they are.

To really get a handle on your resistance score, you may want to give voice to your resistance and express how you want things to be different. What does your resistance sound like in your head? Usually it sounds something like this: *I can't do it. This sucks. This is so unfair. I should… They shouldn't…* In the following space, express your resistance:

_____

_____

_____

_____

_____

_____

Now list three things you could say to yourself or do that would decrease your resistance. Usually this sounds something like this: *I'll give it a try. This is the way it is. Sometimes life is unfair. I will… Even though I'm not happy about, I realize they won't…* Write your new statements here:

1. _____

_____

2. _____

_____

3. _____

_____

Has your resistance level changed? If your resistance is lower, recalculate your suffering score with the equation

$$\text{Suffering} = \text{Pain} \times \text{Resistance}$$

giving yourself the gift of mindfulness

The following practices will support you in befriending your feelings. In time, you will develop the ability to have your feelings without your feelings having you. Acknowledging your feelings with an attitude of kindness and curiosity is often a first step in moving through unpleasant, difficult, and painful situations. Another useful approach is to use the equation Suffering = Pain x Resistance to consider how your habits of thinking and feeling may be increasing your suffering.

* Practice befriending your feelings every day (see chapter 24).

* Bring your kind and curious attention to the thoughts, feelings, and physical sensations that accompany unpleasant events (use the chart in chapter 32).

* Notice how resistance increases suffering (chapter 33).

* Play with ways to decrease your resistance and move forward in painful situations.

* Remember, while we usually can't control the painful events in our lives, we can choose how we respond to them.

Mindfulness is ~

Honest. It asks us to be true to our experience.

part 5

emotions, responding vs. reacting

In part 4, you practiced befriending your feelings, and bringing kind and curious attention to unpleasant events and to how we often increase our own suffering by wanting things to be different. In this part of the book, you'll build on these practices, learning a bit of emotion theory and practicing responding (choosing your behavior) rather than reacting (doing something out of habit or impulse).

chapter 35

Activity:
Understanding Emotion Theory

A psychologist named Paul Ekman has studied emotional expression all over the world, from very developed countries to areas without Internet access or even TVs. His research has shown that all mammals (including us humans) are social creatures and that emotions are an essential part of our lives. In fact, our survival as a species depends on our social relationships and emotional communication.

Dr. Ekman found that there are seven universal emotions that all human beings share. Can you guess what some of the primary emotions are?

_____

_____

_____

_____

_____

_____

_____

_____

_____

Now that you've given it some thought, here are the primary emotions Dr. Ekman identified: happiness, fear, anger, sadness, surprise, contempt, and disgust. All of these emotions serve an evolutionary purpose, helping us survive as a species—detecting threats, dealing with challenges, and connecting with loved ones.

Now consider the seven basic emotions and how each might contribute to our survival.

Which might help us detect threats?

_____

Which might help us deal with challenges?

_____

Which might help us connect with loved ones?

_____

Here are the basics about the functions of our primary emotions:

Fear helps us survive by avoiding danger.

Anger helps us survive by overcoming obstacles.

Happiness helps us connect with our loved ones.

Sadness lets our loved ones know we're upset, so they can comfort us.

Surprise lets our loved ones know we have experienced something new or different.

Contempt and disgust keep us away from potentially toxic experiences.

Dr. Ekman's work also revealed that each of the primary emotions has a very specific facial expression and body presentation. Take a moment now to make each of the following facial movements. Notice how you *feel* as you try each one.

1. Open your eyes wide. Raise your eyebrows, drop your jaw, and open your mouth in an O shape. How do you feel when you make this facial expression? What do you notice in your body? What emotion does this express?

2. Using your cheeks and other facial muscles, gently curve the corners of your mouth up toward the outside corners of your eyes. How do you feel when you make this facial expression? What do you notice in your body? What emotion does this express?

3. Again, using your facial muscles, curve the corners of your mouth down toward your shoulders. How do you feel? What do you notice in your body? What emotion does this express?

What's fascinating is that even though these are small, incomplete versions of the facial expressions that Dr. Ekman described, as you did this exercise, you probably felt a sense of these emotions in your body. For example, when making the facial expression for surprise, you may have felt a little surprised. When smiling, you may have felt a bit happier, and when frowning you may have felt slightly sad. Like the Befriending Feelings practice in chapter 24 and the Emotional Improv activity in chapter 38, this exercise allows us to experience a basic truth—our physical experience and our emotions are very closely connected.

Another interesting thing about emotions is that when we don't suppress or magnify them, they tend to have their own natural rhythm. In your daily life, can you notice when an emotion begins, when it peaks, and when it ends? Based on your experience, how might you graph, or describe, an emotion over time? In most cases, the graph for an emotional experience is like a simple wave or bell curve.

chapter 36

Basic Concept:
Refractory Period

Dr. Ekman uses the term *refractory period* to define the peak of an emotion.

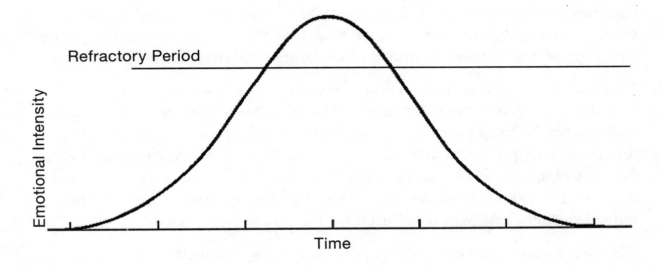

Dr. Ekman's research shows that during the refractory period, we are taken over by the emotion and can't think clearly. In these moments, we're controlled by an older part of the brain (sometimes called the "lizard brain" or "reptilian brain"). When this happens, we're in fight, flight, or freeze mode. This means that, like lizards, we can only fight, run away, or freeze. We aren't able to use our full human minds and hearts to slow down, consider our options, be creative, solve problems...

Take a few minutes to describe a time when you were in the refractory period:

_____

_____

_____

After the refractory period passes, we once again have access to our entire wonderful human mind (and heart). We can look at the big picture, acknowledge what we feel and want, see things from someone else's point of view, consider what they feel and want, and explore creative solutions to various difficulties.

Fortunately, mindfulness can help us notice the beginning of an emotion, the refractory period, and the end of the emotion. Does this progression remind you of anything else you've been mindful of—like the breath, sounds, or thoughts?

After learning about emotion theory, a teen named Alex described watching the progression of his anger as being like watching the lit fuse of a bomb. He said that with practice, he could *sometimes* put out the fuse with the water of mindfulness. Another teen named Justin said that when he began to feel angry, it was like feeling the energy building while waiting in line for a wild, bumpy ride at an amusement park. He also said that when he was aware of this feeling, he could get out of line and not go on the ride (which was usually a big fight with his mom).

When we're *aware* that we're in the grips of an emotion, during the refractory period, we can make very basic choices—at least some of the time. We can pour water on the fuse, step out of the line at the amusement park, or as my son says with a smile, "Shut up and sit there." This is a skill he used often with an annoying carpool companion. We'll return to this idea in chapter 41.

chapter 37

Activity:
Watching Your Emotional Waves

An analogy I like to use is watching waves. Often strong emotions can take us by surprise, like a tsunami. Mindfulness can work like an early warning system. If we're paying attention, we can see the very first ripples of an emotion. Then we can watch the emotional wave get bigger and more powerful. Once we see the wave building, we can choose to step back and move to higher ground so the wave doesn't come crashing down on us. When I work with teens like Alex and Justin, I often ask them to draw the waves of their anger. Here are two examples.

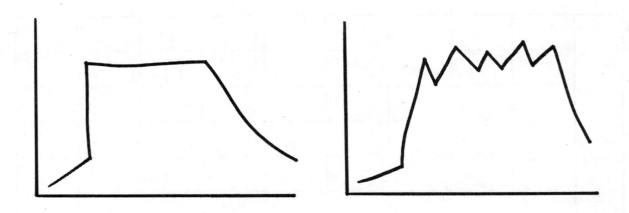

While everyone's emotional waves may vary from day to day, we all tend to have emotional patterns. Draw your usual patterns for the following basic emotions.

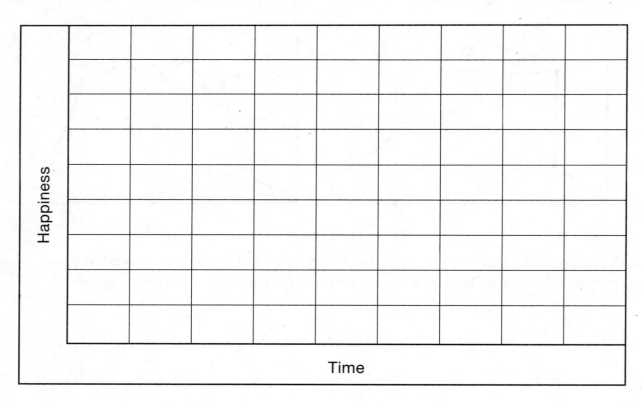

Sadness

Time

Fear

Time

chapter 38

Activity:
Emotional Improv

Knowing your general emotional wave patterns can be very useful. This knowledge allows you to recognize emotions and either move to higher ground or ride out the emotional wave before you act. A key element in being aware of emotional waves is recognizing *how* different emotions show up in your body. Acting out some basic emotions will help you get a feel for this. Even if you are reluctant or want to blow this off, give it a try. Find a private space, maybe a bathroom, your bedroom, or a corner of your yard, where you can do this exercise. Because anger is very common and often problematic, we'll begin with it.

1. Take a moment to rest in stillness, then take one step forward and show a small amount of anger—say 25 percent—with your body and face. Feel what this feels like in your body, mind, and heart…

2. Now step back and rest in stillness. When you're ready, step forward again and show a medium amount of anger—say 50 percent—with your body and face. Feel what this feels like in your body, mind, and heart…

3. Now step back and rest in stillness. When you're ready, step forward again and show a large amount of anger—say 75 percent—with your body and face. Feel what this feels like in your body, mind, and heart… If you feel inspired, you can even add an angry sound.

What happens in your body when you show anger? Describe it, getting into the details of how your legs, arms, hands, chest, and face feel:

_____

_____

_____

_____

_____

What thoughts did you notice when you acted angry, or *embodied* anger?

_____

_____

_____

Is this feeling familiar?

Circle one: Yes.   No.   Sort of.

How often do you feel like this?

Circle one: Often.   Sometimes.   Rarely.

Do you feel awkward or uncomfortable being angry?

Circle one: Yes.   No.   Sometimes.

When you stepped back and rested in stillness, what happened to the emotion? Did it intensify? Fade? Change or remain the same?

Now, act out anger again, only this time just to 5 percent—a smidge of anger... Is there a benefit to knowing what your body feels like when you're just a little bit angry? Could this have anything to do with emotional waves and the refractory period?

Exactly! Knowing that you're *beginning* to get angry is basically an early warning system. If you can notice the initial physical sensations and thoughts near the start of the anger wave, you can often make better choices than when you're really angry and caught in the refractory period.

Consider how noticing that you're beginning to feel angry, and then making a wise choice, might play out for you. List three helpful choices that you could make in almost any situation when you notice you are beginning to get angry:

1. _____

2. _____

3. _____

If you wish, you can repeat the acting exercise with other emotions, perhaps sadness, fear, jealousy, or excitement. I definitely encourage you to end this activity by expressing and embodying as much joy as you can.

chapter 39

Basic Concept:
Wave Theory and Emotional Physics

In real life, emotional patterns and interactions are often extremely complicated, because our waves aren't separate from the waves of others. Instead, our waves usually combine with the waves of others. In fact, in most situations in daily life, like in a family, a group of friends, a classroom, or on a team, there can be many different emotional waves cresting at the same time.

When two big waves peak at the same time, it creates an extremely large, powerful wave. When a big wave and a small wave combine, or when a big wave meets smooth water, the big wave is neutralized, creating calmer waters.

In physics, when two waves combine to create a bigger wave, it's called *constructive interference*. When a big wave combines with a dip or trough and they cancel each other out, it's called *destructive interference*. Sometimes things aren't so simple, and this is called *mixed interference*.

Here are some visual images for these wave combinations, with each line representing the emotions of one person. To further complicate things, a person may have more than one emotion, and there may be multiple people involved. Consider this the next time you're in the middle of a big fight or disagreement.

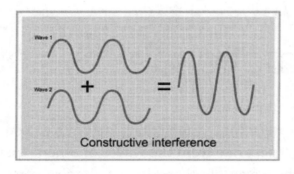

Constructive interference

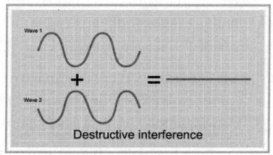

Destructive interference

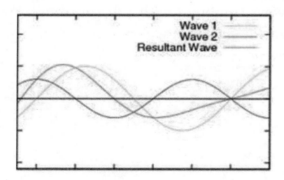

These analogies can be particularly useful during challenging moments with friends and family. At a minimum, when we realize we are in an emotional tsunami, we can move to higher ground and allow the intensity to pass.

chapter 40

Practice:
Stretch and Balance

For this practice, you'll do some simple stretches and balancing exercises. I've described them here, and you'll probably find it easier to do this practice if you download and listen to the guided audio, available at http://www.newharbinger.com/33766.

This practice is about...

* Bringing kind and curious attention to moving your body

* Being curious about how you do something new and unusual

* Understanding that what we call "balance" is actually a series of wobbles and adjustments

* Learning that you can wobble, adjust, and find your balance in other areas of your life

* Listening to and respecting your body

* Being gentle and kind with yourself

* Having fun with a challenge

* Noticing how you talk to yourself

* Working at your limit

* Finding the stillness and quietness within movement

This exercise explores stretching and balancing. As you practice, listen to the wisdom of your body and honor your limits, remembering that limits can change from moment to moment. Sometimes we are more flexible and stable than at other times. This is true not only physically but also mentally and emotionally. So offer kindness to your experience—this body, this mind, and this heart, right here, right now.

Begin by standing with your feet about hip distance apart; feel your feet making contact with the floor, allow your knees to soften, and let your spine lengthen.

Breathe.

Gently roll your left ear toward your left shoulder, feeling the sensations on the left and right sides of your neck and maybe even in the upper back.

Slowly roll your chin toward your chest, breathing, feeling the effects of this movement.

When you are ready, roll your right ear toward your right shoulder.

In your own time, allow your head to return to center.

Breathe.

Gently roll your shoulders up, back, down and forward. Feeling the rhythm of the movement, and the breath…and the changing sensations.

Come to stillness.

Slowly raise your arms above your head. On the next out-breath, reach your hands toward the left, making a smooth arc with your body. Breathing, feeling the stretch along the right side of the body and the compression along the left side. Exploring your limits, sensing if you can stretch just a bit more to the left, or if it would be kind to stretch a bit less.

Return to center.

When you are ready, curve to the right. Perhaps feeling the ribs separate just slightly with each in-breath. Again, stretching a bit more, or not.

Returning to center, breathing.

Placing your hands on your hips and bending your knees. Feeling the sensations in the legs…stretching, pulling, tightening, loosening. Adjusting as your body suggests.

In your own time, gently pull your left elbow back and look over your left shoulder, breathing, exploring this position.

When you are ready, gently twisting to the right, maintaining your attention through the movement from left to right, and into this new position. Maybe discovering stillness and quietness in this position.

And again, returning to center and to stillness. Standing tall and perhaps closing your eyes.

Breathing. Resting. Resting. Breathing.

When you are ready, opening your eyes and focusing on a still point in front of you.

Gently shifting your weight to your right leg, standing tall, and bending your left knee, and pulling it toward your chest with your left hand. Feeling the sensations in the back of the leg, the buttocks, and the lower back. Noticing what is happening in your right foot. Noticing how you are talking to yourself—are you criticizing, comparing, encouraging? Can you be kind?

Release your leg. Shake it out.

In your own time, shifting your weight to your left leg and pulling your right knee into your chest. It is okay to wobble, to touch your foot to the floor, and try again. Breathing. Balancing.

Realizing that balance is not something permanent that we get and keep. It is a continuous series of adjustments: some small, some big. And again this is true not only with physical balance but also with balance in other areas of our lives—like the balance between being independent and being in relationships with family and friends, like the balance between schoolwork and other activities, like the balance between activity and rest.

Again releasing the leg and shaking it out.

This next pose is a bit more challenging. Begin by moving the left corner of your mouth up toward your left ear and the right corner of your mouth up toward your right ear. Noticing the physical sensations, thoughts, and feelings that follow this movement.

For this next position, you may want to support yourself by holding on to the back of a chair or using a nearby wall. When you are ready, focus again on a still point and shift your weight to your right leg. Bend your left knee, and reach back and grab the top of your left foot with your left hand, pulling your heel toward your buttocks, feeling the stretch in the front of the thigh and perhaps in the buttocks and belly. Breathing, balancing, wobbling, stretching, being with the body. Bringing kindness and curiosity to your experience.

And releasing, and, if you need to, turning so that your left hand is closer to the wall. Then shifting your weight to your left leg, and reaching back with your right hand for your right foot. Pulling the foot toward the buttocks, breathing your attention into this position.

Releasing and coming to stillness. Feeling the effects of bringing kind attention to your moving body. Remembering that you can bring this type of attention to any movement—reaching for a glass, opening the refrigerator, pouring something to drink... And every time you bring your attention to the body, you are strengthening your muscle of awareness and discovering the stillness and quietness that exist underneath movement.

107

chapter 41

Activity:
Exploring Common "Holes"
and "Different Streets"

Please read the following poem, by Portia Nelson, slowly, twice. As you do so, bring kindness and curiosity to the thoughts and feelings that appear as you read the poem.

Autobiography in Five Short Chapters

Chapter One
> I walk down the street.
>> There is a deep hole in the sidewalk.
>> I fall in.
>> I am lost… I am helpless.
>>> It isn't my fault…
> It takes forever to find a way out.

Chapter Two
> I walk down the same street.
>> There is a deep hole in the sidewalk.
>> I pretend I don't see it.
>> I fall in again.
> I can't believe I am in this same place.
>> But, it isn't my fault.
> It still takes a long time to get out.

Chapter Three
   I walk down the same street.
      There is a deep hole in the sidewalk.
      I see it is there.
      I still fall in...it's a habit...but,
         my eyes are open.
         I know where I am.
   It is my fault.
   I get out immediately.

Chapter Four
   I walk down the same street.
      There is a deep hole in the sidewalk.
      I walk around it.

Chapter Five
   I walk down another street.

Now ask yourself: Is the woman who wrote the poem talking about a real street with a real hole?

Not really. She's talking about everyday problems and difficulties, especially ones that happen again and again. Do you have any problems or difficulties that seem to come up again and again?

List your top three repetitive problems or difficulties:

1._____

2._____

3._____

Some holes that many teens fall into are listed on the following page. Circle the ones that apply to you.

Sometimes it may feel like we have been pushed into a hole, other times we may push or drag someone else into a hole, and sometimes we can fall into a hole all by ourselves. Take a look at the holes you listed and see which of these descriptions applies to each one.

HOMEWORK AND SCHOOL HOLES

- procrastination
- disorganization
- attacks by unkind mind

SIBLING HOLES

- mean teasing
- frequent fights

FRIENDSHIP HOLES

- feeling excluded or jealous
- going along with something to be "cool"
- not saying what you want
- being mean

PARENT HOLES

- not listening
- not being listened to
- disagreements about responsibilities and privileges

RISK HOLES

- drinking
- using drugs
- driving unsafely
- having unprotected sex
- stealing
- fighting
- participating in gangs
- cutting
- suicidal thinking

chapter 42

Basic Concept:
Responding vs. Reacting

Many teens find that using the image of choosing a "different street" helps them *respond* rather than *react* in difficult situations. *Reacting* is acting automatically, out of habit, usually during the refractory period—in other words, falling into a hole. *Responding* means pausing, breathing, and choosing your behavior—in other words, intentionally walking down a different street. You and your family may find this analogy useful. It may even become a household joke.

I recently worked with a family with three teenage boys. The boys were always provoking each other, getting into dangerous physical fights, and making home life very unpleasant—in other words, pulling each other into holes over and over again. It had gotten so bad that their mother was exhausted and afraid, and the boys and the parents all agreed they needed help. I learned that the usual sequence of events started with one of the boys being bored or angry. Then, rather than dealing with his feelings in a constructive way, he would distract himself by bothering one of his brothers. The end result was usually physical fighting and major emotional upset, which was stressful for everyone.

I asked the family to do an exercise describing one of these incidents. Here's what the two younger teen boys and the mom came up with.

Youngest Boy

Hole: Fighting with my brother

Thoughts: Don't have any

Feelings: Angry, sad

Middle Boy

Hole: *Fighting with my brother*

Thoughts: *I hate him! Leave me alone! Get out of my room!*

Feelings: *ANGRY*

Mom

Hole: *Boys fighting*

Thoughts: *They're at it again. I can't take this. They are out of control. Someone is going to get seriously hurt. It has to stop. I'm a terrible mother.*

Feelings: *Angry, sad, desperate, afraid*

As we discussed the most recent incident, it became clear that, although he hadn't realized it, the youngest brother had been frustrated with his homework. He wasn't aware of what he was feeling, and to relieve the uncomfortable feeling, he went into the middle brother's room and started messing with his stuff, just to bug him. The middle brother had also been somewhat frustrated and bored with his homework, so when his younger brother started bugging him, he did what he usually did: fight with and eventually hurt his younger brother. And when the boys began fighting, their mom started yelling at them.

As we explored the sequence of events, everyone realized that "the street" in their house was one enormous "hole," and that each family member had ways of trying to push the others into it. To make matters worse, each of them fell or jumped into the hole whenever given even the slightest opportunity.

As everyone in the family practiced mindfulness, they became more aware of the thoughts and feelings that caused them to fall into holes. Over time, this allowed them to choose different streets, at least some of the time, and this created a more peaceful home.

Different Streets

Youngest boy: Not bugging him, not letting him bug me, going outside and playing some basketball

Middle boy: *Shutting up and sitting there, telling him I am not going in the hole with him, walking away, asking Mom for help*

Mom: *Getting support for myself by working with Dr. Amy. Practicing responding rather than reacting (yelling). Setting and enforcing clear consequences.*

chapter 43

Activity:
Choosing a Different Street

Using one of your top three repetitive problems or difficulties (see list from chapter 41), complete the following cartoon.

1. Under the heading "Hole Street," briefly describe your problem or difficulty.

2. To the left of the street curving down, list the thoughts that typically appear when you face this difficulty.

3. To the right of the street curving down, list the feelings that typically appear when you face this difficulty.

4. Under the heading "New Street," list three creative new actions, or responses—that are different from what you usually do—that might keep you out of the hole.

Holes and Different Streets

Hole Street

Thoughts

Feelings

New Street

giving yourself the gift of mindfulness

For the next week or so, I encourage you to bring kind and curious attention to your feelings, being aware of when you're in the refractory period and unable to see things clearly and using this important information to pause and respond (choose a different street), rather than react (fall into the hole), in difficult situations.

* Alternate doing the Stretch and Balance practice (chapter 40) and the Befriending Feelings practice (chapter 24).

* Bring kind and curious attention to emotional waves in yourself and others.

* Be aware of the refractory period.

* Practice responding (taking a different street) rather than reacting (falling into a familiar hole).

Mindfulness is ~

Responsive. It helps us choose our behavior.

part 6

responding and communicating

If you've been reading this book from the beginning, you now have a powerful set of tools to help you live a less stressful, more enjoyable life. Here's a quick review. You've learned to rest in stillness and quietness. You've practiced watching your thoughts, befriending your feelings, and decreasing your suffering by letting go of resistance, or wanting things to be different. You've been learning to ride the waves of your emotions. And in part 5, you started practicing responding (taking a different street) rather than reacting (falling into the same old holes). The rest of this book will help you apply these tools to situations in your daily life, and offer guidance on how you can treat yourself and others with genuine kindness and compassion.

chapter 44

Basic Concept:
Almost Moments

Let's start with a simple story about responding rather than reacting, shared by a younger student in one of my courses. We were discussing unpleasant events, and Michael, a fourth grader at a low-income school, reported that his new cat had bitten him, that it hurt, and that he'd wanted to hit the cat. I asked, "Did you?" He smiled and simply said, "No. But I almost did." As a class, we dubbed this an *almost moment*.

For the remaining five weeks of the course, we explored other almost moments— at home, at school, and in life—not hitting the cat at home or the bully on the playground, hanging in there with a difficult math problem or after a disagreement with a friend, and so on. As a teenager, you may face more challenging almost moments: choosing not to cheat to get a better grade, not to use drugs, not to have unprotected sex, not to get in the car with a drunk friend, not to join a gang, or maybe even choosing not to stand in front of a high-speed train.

Maybe some of these examples seem dramatic, or maybe one or more of them feel all too familiar. All of them come from teens I've worked with. Tragically, in 2010 in Palo Alto, the university town just south of where I live, over the course of six months, six teenagers took their lives by standing in front of high-speed trains. Each was probably grappling with extreme feelings of depression and suicidal thoughts like *My life is hopeless, I'd be better off dead*, or *No one cares* (Unkind Mind on steroids). How different might things have been if even one of these teens had learned to explore his or her thoughts and feelings with the curiosity, perspective, and kindness that Michael expressed in his almost moment. We can never know what would have happened. But perhaps they would still be here today, and if someone were to ask them, "Did you stand in front of the train?" they would smile and simply say, "No. But I almost did."

It may be surprising to realize that your life could literally depend on developing the ability to choose wisely and take a different street in the intense almost moments, when things feel unbearably difficult.

chapter 45

Basic Concept:
You Will Always See

In Michael's class that day (see chapter 44), the discussion of almost moments shifted to a conversation about getting caught—and often punished—when we aren't able to pause, when we miss the almost moment, react, and fall into a hole. This, in turn, led to a discussion about guilt and the experience of feeling guilty, even if we aren't caught. The conversation prompted me to share a well-known story with the group.

Once upon a time, on the outskirts of a big city, there stood an old school. From a young age, girls and boys would come to live in the school and to learn from the teacher. One day the teacher who ran this small school decided to teach her students a lesson. She gathered them around her and spoke: "My dear students, as you can see, I am growing old and slow. I can no longer provide for the needs of the school as I once did. I know I have not yet taught you to work for money, and so I can think of only one thing that can keep our school from closing.

"Our nearby city is full of wealthy people with more money in their purses than they could ever need. I want you to go into the city and follow those rich people as they walk through the crowded streets, or when they walk down the deserted alleyways. When no one is looking, and *only when no one is looking,* you must steal their purses from them. That way we will have enough money to keep our school alive." (At this point, Michael and many of his classmates gasped and shook their heads.)

"But Teacher," the students chorused in disbelief, "you have taught us that it is wrong to take anything that does not belong to us."

"Yes, indeed I have," the old teacher replied. "It would be wrong to steal if it were not absolutely necessary. And remember, you must not be seen! If *anyone* can see you, you must not steal! Do you understand?"

The students looked nervously from one to another. Had their beloved teacher gone mad? "Yes, Teacher," they said quietly.

"Good," she said. "Now go, and remember, you must not be seen!" The students got up and left the school building. The old teacher rose slowly and watched them go. When she returned to her seat, she saw that one student was still standing quietly in the corner of the room. "Why did you not go with the others?" she asked the girl. "Don't you want to help save our school?"

"I do, Teacher," said the girl quietly. "But you said that we had to steal without being seen. I know that there is no place on Earth that I would not be seen, for I would always see myself."

"Excellent!" exclaimed the teacher. "That is just the lesson that I hoped you and the others would learn, but you were the only one to see it. Run and tell your friends to return to the school before they get us into trouble." The girl ran and got her friends, who were nervously gathered just out of sight of the school, trying to decide what to do. When they returned, the teacher told them the words the girl had spoken, and they all understood the lesson.

What does this story have to do with our discussion about holes and almost moments, and choosing our behavior?

No matter what we do, we always have a mindful part of ourselves that is quietly watching and that can guide us if we can pause and listen.

chapter 46

Practice:
Body Scan

Bringing your kind and curious attention to your body can be extremely helpful, especially when you're feeling overwhelmed by intense emotions or experiencing an Unkind Mind attack. Paying attention to your body in this way can help you be in the moment, right here, right now, and not be stuck in your thinking about tomorrow or yesterday. Again, the easiest way to do this practice (at least in the beginning) is to download the audio from http://www.newharbinger.com/33766. Otherwise, you may want to read through the entire practice and then give it a try, or alternatively, you can read and follow the suggestions a couple of paragraphs at a time.

So let's bring some kind attention to the body. Sit or lie in a comfortable position. If you feel comfortable, allow your eyes to close, or if not, then focus on a spot in front of you.

Allow your arms to rest by your sides, and if your legs are crossed, uncross them.

On the next in-breath, feel your back lengthen and straighten. On the next out-breath, allow your muscles to soften. And bring your attention to the familiar expansion and release of the breath in the belly.

Let your attention rest on the rhythm of the breath. To help yourself pay attention to the breath, you may want to place one hand on your belly and the other on your chest…*feeling* the rhythm of the breath and maybe noticing how your body, mind, and heart respond to this simple touch…

When you are ready, let your hands rest in your lap or at your sides, and breathe your kind and curious attention into your feet. Notice the sensations in your feet—the feel of your socks, your shoes, or, if you are barefoot, the air.

Perhaps you can be aware of the spaces between your toes? Perhaps you can feel the sensations in the muscles and bones of your feet?

Now, allow the breath and the attention to move up into the ankles and lower legs. Noting the sensations in the ankles, and feeling the curve of the calf muscles and straightness of the shinbones…

When you are ready, breathe your attention into the knees. Feeling the muscles and tendons that move and support the knees, and then feeling into the knee joints…

Breathing and noticing—the sensations in the knees—and perhaps noticing any thoughts or feelings that happen to be here, now—restlessness, peace, sleepiness, irritation… Letting it all be, just as it is.

And in your own time, breathing the attention into the backs of your thighs and buttocks, feeling the places where your legs make contact with the chair, the floor, or the bed, and the places where they don't. Allowing the attention to circle around the outer thighs, over the tops of the thighs, and across the inner thighs. Perhaps you can feel the weight of your clothing and the specific sensations in the different areas of the thighs.

And now, breathing your attention into the bowl of your pelvis, the area where your legs connect with your body. Perhaps you can feel the breath expanding and releasing in the bowl of your pelvis.

Now again focus your attention on the familiar rising and falling of the breath in your belly. Resting deeply in the stillness and quietness between the in-breaths and the out-breaths.

Allowing the breath and attention to sink through the belly into the lower back. Seeing if you can feel the breath expanding and releasing in the lower back. Experiment with simply noticing what is happening in your body—sensations of tension, comfort, or perhaps *neutrality*, which is a kind of nothingness.

Now, letting the breath and the attention move upward into the mid and upper back, exploring the region between the shoulder blades.

When your attention is pulled by a thought or feeling, gently, kindly, return your attention to the instructions.

When you are ready, allow the breath and attention to move around and through the rib cage into the chest. Again feeling the movement and sensations of the breath in the chest.

Now, letting the breath and attention drift up into the shoulders, and down along the length of your arms into your hands. Noting any sensations of ache, strength, and comfort in the arms. Exploring the sensations in the palms of the hands and the back of the hands, and the fingers and thumbs.

And now moving the breath and attention into the neck, feeling along the back of the neck, the sides of the neck, the front of the neck. Perhaps even feeling the movement of the breath in the throat.

Now, allow the breath and the attention to move up into your face, feeling the position of your jaw, the curve of your lips, and your facial expression.

Perhaps you can feel the breath moving in and out at the tip of your nose, and the touch of your hair, or the air on your forehead?

Let the breath and attention circle along the sides of the head, to the back of the head, up to the top of the head, and into the brain… Again, just noting the sensations as you breathe kind attention into your face, head, and brain.

Now let breath and attention fill your entire body—brain, head, face, neck, arms, chest, back, belly, pelvis, legs, and feet.

Feeling the breath filling you and emptying you.

Appreciating the stillness and quietness and aliveness inside of you.

Perhaps taking a moment to be grateful for this body, this one that is here right now, exactly as it is…

And as this session comes to an end, it can be helpful to remember that bringing kind and curious attention to the body can help us, especially during difficult times. Anytime you find yourself stuck in thinking or upset by feelings, you can bring your attention to the body in very short, simple, secret ways. You can notice the sensations of breathing, the feeling of your feet on the floor, the weight of your backpack on your shoulders, or the shape of the pencil in your hand. Often, choosing to drop your attention out of your head and into your belly or your feet can interrupt repetitive patterns of negative thoughts and feelings and decrease their intensity.

Being mindful of the body is one way to drop into the Still Quiet Place.

chapter 47

Reflection:
Body Scan

What was it like to bring your attention into your body?

_____

_____

_____

What did you discover about how your body is in this moment?

_____

_____

_____

How do your mind and heart feel, now that you have given your body some kind and curious attention?

_____

_____

_____

chapter 48

Activity:
Difficult Communication

When we're upset in the heat of the moment—at the peak of the refractory period—we often react and just blurt out thoughts and feelings as they appear. If the person we're interacting with does the same thing, we soon find ourselves tossed about on huge waves of reactivity, drowning in a shared tsunami of thoughts and feelings.

In this activity, you'll recall a difficult interaction with someone, and use the accompanying cartoon to write about what you and the other person were feeling and wanting, and explore creative solutions that might help—or have helped—the two of you resolve the disagreement.

Difficult Communication Exercise

I feel, I want

Creative Solutions

I feel, I want

Take several slow, deep breaths, settling into stillness and quietness. Then remember a difficult discussion you had this week—a disagreement with a classmate, friend, family member, teacher, or someone else.

Once you have a clear memory of the interaction, you can fill in the cartoon. The first step in the process of communicating skillfully is to ask yourself, *What did I feel? And what did I want?* When you've brought to mind how you felt and what you wanted in the situation you have remembered, write it down. It's fine to sum it up in just a few brief words or phrases.

Sometimes the answers to these questions are quick and clear. At other times, it may be helpful to slow down and *really* listen to what was true for you. Before moving on to the next step, it's important to understand your emotions and your desires.

The second step is considering what the other person felt and wanted. This is the step people are tempted to skip. Yet without this step, it's often difficult, if not impossible, to communicate and move toward a solution. So, for just a few moments, let go of what you felt and wanted and *really* consider what the other person felt and wanted. When you truly "get" the other person's experience, write a few brief words or phrases describing it on the cartoon.

Now that you have a better understanding of what both you and the other person wanted and felt, the third step is to consider how you might have gotten out of this hole. What different streets could you have chosen? Were there any creative solutions you overlooked? If you have some ideas, write them down. If you feel stuck, consider talking to a friend or trusted adult about possible solutions.

You may think, *Screw this! I don't care.* Yet if you were riled up and upset, it's likely that you did actually care. Maybe you just cared about getting what you wanted, which would be totally normal. Or maybe you cared about the person you were arguing with. Or maybe, as is often the case, you cared about both.

In difficult interactions, the combination of paying attention to our own feelings and desires and considering the feelings and desires of others helps us be kinder to ourselves and to those we're dealing with. Sometimes we can do this only after the fact; *sometimes,* if we are really practicing mindfulness, we can slow down and do this process in real time. If either after the fact or in real time, things have gotten off to a bad start or gotten out of hand, we may need to walk away, cool down, or just take a deep breath and begin again in the moment—pausing, moving through the described steps, and then saying something like, "Hey, we got off to a bad start. Can we start over? I'm really doing my best to share what's important to me with you, *and* to *hear* what's important to you, so that we can come up with something that works for both of us. Can we slow down and try this again?"

As you continue to practice mindful communication, try not to rush the process. Really take your time to understand what's true for you and for the other person. For example, if a friend has rejected you, you might be tempted to pretend you don't care. However, your truth may be *I feel hurt, sad, confused, and angry. And even though this person continues to be unkind to me, I still want to be friends.* It can be scary and feel vulnerable to admit how you really feel and what you really want, even if you're only admitting it to yourself.

You may be surprised by what you discover when you take the time to understand what's really true. You might realize that you really don't want to be friends with this person. You might see that the other person feels insecure and doesn't know how to be your friend. Or you may find that as much as you truly want to be friends, the other person doesn't want to be friends with you.

Even if you don't like what you discover, acknowledging what you feel and want and what the other person feels and wants provides you with the information you need to consider your choices. For example, if you understand that you want to be friends and that the other person is, at best, unsure about being friends, you have several options. You may choose to reach out to the other person and see what happens. You may choose to be a true friend to yourself, treating yourself with the kindness and respect that you absolutely deserve, and letting go of pursuing a friendship with this person. And you may choose to seek out other friends. The choice is yours. However, if you realize that the other person is actually being cruel, or bullying, please seek the support of a trusted adult.

chapter 49

Practice: Difficult Communication with Parents

As a teen, much of your difficult communication may be with your parents. As a parent, some of my most difficult communication is with my teens. Usually, these difficulties are because underneath whatever true craziness is going on, we really love each other. And it is the people we love who are most likely to get under our skin, push our buttons, piss us off.

So if you have a difficult topic that you wish to discuss with your parents—a poor grade; breaking a family, school, or even a legal rule; sexual activity; drug use; wanting some space and the opportunity to do things your own way; needing your parents to step up and offer more support; choosing your own path rather than the one they set out for you—the following practice could help.

As with other practices, this may feel awkward and overly structured at first. And especially if you and your parents are repeatedly falling into a hole about a particular topic, practicing discussing things using a new, intentional structure can be extremely helpful.

In this moment, you and your parents may be in a deep hole, or things may be fine, or even great. No matter how it is, I encourage you to share the following letter with your parents *now*. Then the next time there is something difficult to discuss, everyone will be prepared to practice a new way of communicating, understand the basics of the process, and have agreed to use this structure.

To introduce this new way of communicating to your parents, you can use the letter on the next page, filling in the blanks and giving them a copy or reading it to them from the book, or simply sharing the process with them in your own words. If you choose the last option, make sure you include all the steps.

Dear Parents,

I have been reading a mindfulness workbook and practicing—breathing, slowing down, being aware of thoughts, feelings, and physical sensations, circumstances, impulses, and interactions, and, most importantly, using this information to respond *rather than* react *to various situations. (Responding is pausing and choosing behavior. Reacting is acting out of habit and upset.)*

I am now inviting you to practice these skills too, in discussing _____ (a difficult topic). Since this is a loaded topic, I am asking that we try something new, and we agree to use this format, which is specifically designed to enhance listening and understanding.

To begin, I will have _____ minutes (an agreed-upon time) to simply share my view, feelings, experience, and requests. I will use I-statements, *rather than accusations. You will* listen *and, to the best of your ability, not interrupt, disagree, express your concerns, or make your case either out loud or silently to yourself. Again, to the best of your ability, you will simply listen with your* heart *to what I have to say.*

Then we will have a cooling off period of _____ minutes/days (an agreed-upon time). Before *you share your* response, *you will summarize what you heard me say and allow me to clarify anything that you have misinterpreted.*

Then, you will have _____ minutes to simply share your view, feelings, experience, and requests. I will listen *and, to the best of my ability, not interrupt, disagree, express my concerns, or make my case either out loud or silently to myself. Again, to the best of my ability, I will simply listen with my* heart *to what you have to say.*

Then, after another cooling off period of _____ minutes/days, we will have a slow, mindful two-way conversation. Anytime someone feels things are getting heated, he or she may use a time-out signal, and we will all pause and take five full, slow, deep breaths.

Before we begin to practice this new way of communicating, we acknowledge that we may fall into old patterns, that developing new habits takes time, and that we still may not agree or find a mutually acceptable solution. The intention of this practice is to support us in hearing and understanding each other during our most difficult moments.

The essential elements of the process are that the speaker *(the person initiating the conversation) agrees to share his or her view, feelings, experience, and requests, using "When you...I feel" statements rather than accusations. (Teen: "When you tell me to try harder, and I am really trying, I feel hopeless and alone." Parent: "When you don't respond to my texts, I feel worried and frustrated.") Note: Feelings are variations of mad, sad, glad, afraid, hurt, lonely... You can find a useful chart of feelings can be found at www.cnvc .org/sites/default/files/feelingsinventory0.pdf. Also note also that "I feel that you..." and "I feel like you..." are accusations, not feelings.*

The listener *agrees to listen from the heart, listen without interrupting, disagreeing, or expressing concerns, listen without making counterarguments, either out loud or silently, and after an agreed-upon pause of at least forty-five minutes, summarize what he or she has heard and understood, and ask for clarification.*

Everyone agrees to breathe and to watch his or her own thoughts, feelings, physical sensations, and assumptions...as they appear... And when things get heated, to pause, breathe, begin again, have a sense of humor, and renew the commitment to really hearing each other and coming up with creative solutions.

If we aren't able to manage the conversation on our own, we will seek support from a wise friend, or a trained professional.

Love,

_____

A note to parents from Dr. Amy:

Dear Parents,

Your teen has wisely chosen to begin practicing mindfulness and courageously invited you to develop new and more effective ways of communicating. I encourage you to **pause** *here and fully commit to doing this practice* **wholeheartedly** *with your teen the next time you address a difficult topic. I know for myself that I am most likely to not hear my kids and to force my own view when, underneath whatever rational argument I am making, I am concerned or afraid about my children's well-being and the* **potential future negative** *impact of their choices.*

When I am mindful, I can be aware of my concerns, fears, and desire to control, and then breathe, and listen, listen, listen, without preparing my counter arguments. Then when I have truly heard my teen, I can begin to look at potential solutions... and **sometimes** *my response remains a simple parental "No." This process minimizes the possibly that I will just dictate how things will go, without first truly hearing and understanding my teen.*

chapter 50

Practice:
THINK! Before Texting or Posting

While on the subject of responding and communicating, let's explore mindful texting and posting on social media. Most teens I know text and post on social media many times each day. While these are great ways to stay in touch with friends, sometimes being able to reply so quickly causes problems. It's always wise to use the acronym THINK before you text, post, or even speak. Fortunately, social media is also a source of wisdom. There are many artistic versions of this practice floating around on the web, so you may already be familiar with it.

Before you speak:

THINK!

T — is it true?

H — is it helpful?

I — is it inspiring?

N — is it necessary?

K — is it kind?

I like to add an exclamation point at the end—THINK!—to encourage people to pause and consider a couple of additional questions:

Would you want a friend or acquaintance to post a similar comment, photo, or video about you?

Would you feel good about your mother, grandma, little brother or sister, school principal, or future employer seeing your comment, photo, or video?

Using the THINK! practice before speaking, texting, or posting can prevent you from putting words and images out into the world that you will later regret.

chapter 51

Basic Concept: Acceptance, or We Can't Always Get What We Want

Particularly during difficult communications, it is helpful to remember that much as we each wish we could get everything we want in life, the reality is that we can't. I can't always get what I want. You can't always get what you want, and others can't always get what they want either. There are definitely times when it's unwise to compromise and other times when no solution can come close to satisfying everyone. In these situations, it's best to pause and really listen for what's true for you. In certain situations, maybe what you thought you wanted isn't what you really want. In other situations, you may find peace by accepting things the way they are. The equation in chapter 33 can be rewritten as Happiness = Pain x Acceptance. The more we are able to accept things as they are, the happier or, at least, the wiser we will be. When we know that our ex isn't coming back, or that we really are moving out of state, or that our dog is dead, we can take as much time as we need to grieve and heal, and gradually move forward.

giving yourself the gift of mindfulness

This week's practice is about responding rather than reacting, choosing a different street, and digging yourself out of holes during difficult communications with others. So when you find yourself in a difficult interaction hole—or, better yet, before you find yourself all the way down at the bottom—take a few moments to consider what you feel and want, what the other person feels and wants, and possible compromises or solutions.

* Use the simple three-step process in the Difficult Communication activity (chapter 48) anytime you have a difficult interaction or anticipate one.

* Practice the Body Scan (chapter 46) every day.

Mindfulness is ~

Powerful. It can transform our communication.

part 7

choice and kindness

In this part of the book, we'll continue to explore the advantage of responding—*choosing* your actions—rather than reacting. We'll take a closer look at almost moments—the space between impulse and action—and learn about four common ways of dealing with times when we feel threatened. Additionally, we'll play with some fun mnemonics—acronyms or memory devices that tie everything we've been practicing together into easily remembered steps. And you will begin practicing loving-kindness for yourself and others.

chapter 52

Basic Concept:
Impulses

In my groups both with younger children and with teens, I often let them kick back and chill while I read a short children's story titled "Paul," from the book *Sideways Stories from Wayside School,* by Louis Sachar. This story is a conversation between Paul and temptation. It's about noticing urges and choosing whether to act on them. It offers a humorous take on almost moments and holes and different streets—in other words, responding versus reacting.

Briefly, temptation encourages Paul to pull Leslie's pigtails. He has an extended conversation with temptation. Initially, he is able to resist; then, ultimately, he pulls Leslie's pigtails, first the left and then the right. After each pull, Leslie yells that Paul pulled her pigtail, and Paul gets a check mark by his name on the blackboard. Then Leslie yells again (although it is clear that Paul didn't actually pull her pigtail a third time). He gets a third check mark by his name and is sent home early on the kindergarten bus.

chapter 53

Activity:
Impulses

While this may seem like a dorky kindergarten example, we all have times when we have an impulse to do something unkind or sneaky, like steal something, lie, gossip, or cheat on a test.

Being honest and courageous with yourself, list one time when you had an impulse to do something unkind or sneaky. Remember that a part of you is quietly watching, and you will always see (chapter 45).

_____

_____

_____

_____

When you had that impulse, did you hear a voice in your head saying, *No! Wait! What am I doing? I'll only get into trouble*?

Circle one: Yes.   No.   Maybe.

Did you hear another voice that said, *It's no big deal. No one will ever know*?

Circle one: Yes.   No.   Maybe.

How might being able to notice these impulses and voices help you?

_____

_____

_____

_____

Why is it sometimes so hard to listen to your wise, kind voice and take a different street?

_____

_____

_____

_____

chapter 54

Activity:
Choosing How to Respond to Impulses

In a moment, you're going to read a word. Immediately after you read the word, notice what happens in your body and your mind. Do your best to just notice without doing anything or making any movements.

Okay, here's the word: itch.

What did you notice?

_____

Were you suddenly aware of an itch that you weren't aware of before?

Circle one: Yes.   No.

Were you able to notice the itch without scratching it?

Circle one: Yes.   No.

If you did scratch the itch, were you able to notice the impulse to scratch before you actually scratched?

Circle one: Yes.   No.

Did you notice any thoughts that came along with the impulse—before you scratched? If so, what were they?

_____

_____

_____

Did you maybe think, *Oh, just one scratch…nobody will ever know*, or *It doesn't matter if I scratch*? Whatever you thought is fine. This isn't about being good or bad, right or wrong. It's about bringing kind and curious attention to your body, your thoughts, and your feelings and then choosing your actions.

Isn't it interesting that just one little word can produce sensations in your body, and that those sensations can lead to thoughts and urges, and that those urges can lead to actions?

And if you think about it, "itch" is such a simple word. What do you suppose might happen with other words? As you scan the following words, pause on each one, and simply notice your thoughts and impulses.

What might this exercise about impulses have to do with social media and advertising? As you probably know, the words and images in social media and advertising create thoughts, impulses, and actions, just like the word "itch." Now consider whether social media and advertising tend to trigger certain kinds of thoughts...

Desire, Unkind Mind, insecurity, FOMO (fear of missing out), to name just a few. It can be helpful to remember this and observe your thoughts and impulses in response to social media or advertising. Then you can choose if you want to spend your time feeling left out, post a nasty reply on social media, spend your money on a particular brand of jeans, or choose another street.

chapter 55

Activity:
Hook Report

In this activity, you'll write a brief book report. To start, just notice any thoughts and feelings that appeared when you read that first sentence. Did you think, *Ugh, why is this mindfulness person making me write a book report? I'm not doing it.* If I were you, I probably would have thought the same thing. However, this short book report is really a hook report—a story about a time when you got hooked by someone or something—when somebody or something pushed your buttons. Can you think of a time in the last couple of days when you got hooked by something? Maybe you lost your real book report because your computer crashed. Maybe a friend made a snarky comment about your outfit. Imagine the situation in detail, then answer the following questions.

Who are the main characters in this story?

_____

_____

What was the hook? In other words, what pushed your buttons?

_____

_____

_____

What did you feel and want?

_____

_____

What did the other characters feel and want?

_____

_____

_____

What ended up happening?

_____

_____

_____

Describe some other possible endings:

_____

_____

_____

_____

Looking back, what would your wisest self have done?

_____

_____

_____

_____

_____

_____

_____

chapter 56

Activity:
Aikido

Aikido is a martial art in which the practitioner enters and blends with an attacker's energy to redirect it. This exercise explores various responses to feeling like you're being attacked. To get into that headspace, imagine that someone is coming at you looking angry and yelling insults or criticisms. Notice the thoughts and feelings that come up as you imagine this.

In general, there are four basic ways people respond when threatened. Can you guess what they are? A good place to start may be simply noticing your own reaction when you imagined being attacked. Write your ideas about the four ways of reacting:

_____

_____

_____

_____

The four responses are described next. You can also see me acting out the responses at http://www.newharbinger.com/33766. As you read the descriptions, watch the video, or both, bring kind and curious attention to your thoughts, feelings, and physical sensations.

Submissive: As the hostile person approaches, you cower to the floor with a fearful expression on your face and posture that says, *Please don't hurt me!*

What were your thoughts, feelings, and physical sensations as you imagined or watched this response?

Thoughts: _____

_____

Feelings: _____

_____

Physical sensations: _____

_____

What might the submissive person be thinking and feeling?

_____

_____

What might the hostile person approaching be thinking and feeling about this submissive response?

_____

_____

When have you felt like the submissive person?

_____

_____

When have you felt like the hostile person?

_____

_____

What situations cause you to react or respond submissively?

_____

_____

Before moving on to the next scenario, take a few slow, deep breaths and allow yourself to reset.

Avoidant: As the hostile person approaches, you simply step out of the way with a casual, *See ya* expression.

What were your thoughts, feelings, and physical sensations as you imagined or watched this response?

Thoughts: _____

_____

Feelings: _____

_____

Physical sensations: _____

_____

What might the avoidant person be thinking and feeling?

_____

_____

What might the hostile person approaching be thinking and feeling about this avoidant response?

_____

_____

When have you felt like the avoidant person?

_____

_____

What situations cause you to react or respond like the avoidant person?

_____

_____

Before moving on to the next scenario, take a few slow, deep breaths and allow yourself to reset.

Aggressive: As the person approaches, you push back forcefully with an angry expression on your face and a *You wanna go?* attitude.

What were your thoughts, feelings, and physical sensations as you imagined or watched this response?

Thoughts: _____

_____

Feelings: _____

_____

Physical sensations: _____

_____

What might the aggressive person being approached be thinking and feeling?

_____

_____

What might the hostile person approaching be thinking and feeling about this aggressive response?

_____

_____

When have you felt like the aggressive person being approached?

_____

_____

What situations cause you to react or respond like the aggressive person being approached?

_____

_____

Before moving on to the next scenario, take a few slow, deep breaths and allow yourself to reset.

Assertive: As the person approaches, you take her outstretched arm and, moving with her, turn her 180 degrees, with a calm expression on your face.

What were your thoughts, feelings, and physical sensations as you imagined or watched this response?

Thoughts: _____

_____

Feelings: _____

_____

Physical sensations: _____

_____

What might the assertive person being approached be thinking and feeling?

_____

_____

What might the hostile person approaching be thinking and feeling about this assertive response?

_____

_____

When have you felt like the assertive person being approached?

_____

_____

What situations cause you to react or respond like the assertive person being approached?

_____

_____

Take a few slow, deep breaths and allow yourself to reset.

chapter 57

Basic Concept:
Aikido

The Aikido activity in chapter 56 is yet another way of looking at responding versus reacting, which you have previously explored in the Holes and Different Streets, Difficult Communication, and Hook Report activities.

This is not meant to suggest that the assertive way is the preferred, right, or better way to respond. In my experience, it's helpful to look at these behaviors along a continuum, from submissive to avoidant to assertive to aggressive. For me, true mindfulness is skillfully *choosing* what is called for, moment by moment. Sometimes it is wise to be submissive. Sometimes a certain amount of clear, forceful energy is called for. However, if we are not mindful, we react out of habit, doing what we always do, trying to please or dominate others. The invitation is simply to recognize our usual ways of behaving and practice *choosing* our responses wisely, based on the circumstances.

One man's amazing response to being threatened is described in a story, reported on National Public Radio, that challenges our preconceptions about when submission, avoidance, assertion, or aggression might be called for.

> A tough teen approached a man, pulled out a knife, and demanded the man's wallet.
> Pause here and consider what you would have done if you were the man…
> In all honesty, if I were in such a situation, as a petite five-foot-one-inch woman, I would have acted submissively, given the teen my wallet and my wedding ring, and begged him not to hurt me.
> In this case, the man handed over his wallet. As the teen walked away, the man called out and offered his jacket and then invited the teen for dinner. The teen accepted, paid for dinner with the man's money, and returned the man's

wallet. The man then offered him twenty dollars in return for the knife. (To read this true story in its entirety, visit npr.org and search for "a victim treats his mugger right.")

I am not implying that this man's response is the *right* way to handle this situation, or that any particular response is good or bad, right or wrong, better or worse. The intention in sharing this story is to explore our habitual responses and skillful alternatives. There may be powerful responses that never even cross our minds. And often what we are first inclined to do is not so helpful.

chapter 58

Practice:
Responding in the Moment

As you may recall from the beginning of the book, my definition of mindfulness is paying attention here and now, with kindness and curiosity, so that we can choose our behavior. In this chapter, I'll give you three mnemonics to support you in bringing mindfulness to moments in your life. The first is a short practice, the second is a medium-length practice, and the third is a longer one. Choose the practice that you feel is most supportive, given the specific circumstances, the timing, and the intensity of the situation.

ABCs

In life, it helps to remember your ABCs, the basics of mindfulness, to help you observe your experience and respond. This is especially true when things are difficult. So when things are difficult, keep these ABCs in mind:

A = Attention

B = Breath

C = Choice

Anytime you want to be more mindful, stop for a moment and pay attention (A) to your breath (B). When you do this, you're much more likely to be successful in choosing (C) a skillful response that's kind to yourself and kind to others.

STAR

I originally created the STAR acronym at the request of teachers to help students who were anxious about taking the annual California Standardized Testing and Reporting (STAR) tests; it's also useful in other challenging situations:

S = Stop.

T = Take a breath.

A = Accept.

R = Resume.

Let's walk through this step-by-step:

Stop. When you're faced with a difficulty, whether it's a test question you don't know the answer to or any difficulty in life, the first step is to stop.

Take a breath. Usually, taking a few slow, deep breaths will relax your mind and body, allowing for the next step.

Accept. Accept that you're having difficulty and that you're a bit stressed. (You might, as one student did, remember this A as *All's well.*)

Resume. When you're ready, after you've taken some slow, deep breaths and accepted things, you can resume, trying again to solve the problem or moving on to something else and coming back to the difficulty a bit later.

Remember, this practice can be used with a difficult problem on a test or homework and also with other difficulties in your life.

PEACE

PEACE stands for

P = Pause.

E = Exhale.

A = Acknowledge, accept, and allow.

C = Choose, with clarity, courage, compassion, and comedy.

E = Engage.

This practice is relatively long and detailed. (A spoken version can be found on the CD *Still Quiet Place: Mindfulness for Teens*, available through iTunes or Amazon.) As you practice it repeatedly, you'll eventually remember the basic elements. You'll also naturally tune in to the aspects of the practice that will be most helpful in a given situation.

As with the ABCs and STAR practices, this one can help you deal with difficult situations, from everyday issues, like losing your cell phone, to more extreme problems like failing a class, breaking up with a girlfriend or boyfriend, having a friend go to jail, or maybe even going to jail yourself, getting pregnant, or grieving a death in your family or community.

Mindfulness is much more than just watching the breath. For me, the power and beauty of mindfulness is that it helps me when things are most difficult.

PEACE is an acronym for a practice that can be used in any difficult situation. As you do this practice for the first time, bring to mind a current problem that you're experiencing. If possible, choose a small issue to begin with—a minor irritation. If you are dealing with something more intense, take your time, go slow, be gentle, and seek support if you need it. Next, read through the steps slowly, pausing after each letter in the mnemonic to follow the suggestions:

P is for pause. When you realize that things are difficult, pause.

E is for exhale. When you exhale, you may want to let out a sigh or a groan. You may even want to cry. That's okay. And after you exhale, you want to…? Inhale. Just keep breathing…

A is for acknowledge, accept, and allow. As you continue to breathe, *acknowledge* the situation as it is. Maybe your backpack with all your stuff is gone, your parents are getting divorced, or your best friend is now dating the person you just broke up with. Acknowledging a situation doesn't mean you're happy about it. It just means that you recognize the situation is what it is, whether you like it or not… A is also for *accept*—accepting the situation and your reaction to it, whether you're feeling furious, devastated, heartbroken, jealous, all of the above, or something else… Finally, A is also for *allowing* your experience. Do your best to rest in the Still Quiet Place and watch all of your thoughts, feelings, and body sensations. Notice whether you're tempted to suppress your experience by pretending that you're fine. Notice if you want to create additional drama by rehashing things in your head or with friends. See if you can allow these tendencies too. See if you can discover a middle way—a way of having your thoughts and feelings without your thoughts and feelings having you and making you act in ways you may regret.

C is for choose. When you're ready—and this may take a few moments, days, weeks, or even months, depending on the situation—choose how you'll respond. At its best, responding involves some additional Cs: clarity, courage, compassion, and comedy. Clarity is being clear about what you want, what your limits are, and what you're responsible for. Courage means being brave about speaking your truth and hearing the truth of others. Compassion means being kind toward yourself and others and understanding how incredibly difficult it sometimes is to be a human being. As for comedy, the word "humor" might be a better fit, but it doesn't start with C… It's amazing how helpful it can be to have a sense of humor and to not take yourself or your situation too seriously.

E is for engage. After you've paused, exhaled, allowed your experience, and chosen your response, you're ready to engage with people, with the situation, and with life.

Now that you've practiced PEACE, you can use this in other real-life situations. For extreme circumstances, you may need to repeat the practice many times a day, *and* you may also want to seek support from a friend, a parent, a teacher, a counselor, or a doctor.

chapter 59

Practice:
Loving-Kindness

Everyone wants to be treated with kindness; we all want to be understood and loved. Yet in our society, we're often focused on *doing* and *getting*—the classes we are taking, the sports we play, the activities we're involved in, the jobs we do, our social lives and social media, getting good grades, getting into trouble, getting the coolest new phone, jeans, concert tickets.… The list goes on and on. In our media-driven frenzy, we often completely forget about less obvious and more important things, like giving and receiving kindness and love.

We almost never think of giving and receiving kindness and love as skills we can learn and practice. Yet we can practice them, and doing so can actually fill the sense of emptiness and desperate ache that drives so much of our other behavior. So practice now. You can read through the following instructions, or you can download and listen to the Loving-Kindness guided audio (available at http://www .newharbinger.com/33766).

Take your time to read and feel your way through this passage. Go slow and let the words settle into your heart:

> Take a few slow, deep breaths and remember a moment when you felt that someone saw you for who you really are, understood you, cared for you, loved you.
>
> The person could be a family member, a coach, a teacher, a mentor, a friend, a pet, or even a stranger in a moment of need…
>
> *Pick someone*, imagine their face, their smile and their laugh, imagine just sitting and being with them…
>
> If at first you don't remember a moment, don't struggle; just breathe and let a moment appear from your memory. It doesn't have to be big or special; it can

be very simple—a kind word, a smile, or a hand on your shoulder. (If no specific memory comes, simply allow a feeling of being loved to wash over you.)

Notice how this feels in your body. What does it feel like to remember being with someone you know understands, cares for, loves you?

Breathing, opening, and *receiving* the gift of kindness and caring. *Take your time. There's no rush.*

Silently, with your mind and heart, send kind wishes to the person (or animal) you've remembered, perhaps saying *May you be happy.*

And *feel* their kindness, caring, love, coming back to you.

When you are ready, offer the same loving wish to yourself, saying *May I be happy.*

Now, remember another moment when someone else cared for or loved you; see their face, hear their voice and their laughter, feel their kindness, caring, and love, and send them a wish saying *May you be happy.*

Let these memories help you really feel the *truth,* that *you are worthy of care and love, that you are truly loveable.*

When you are ready, again offer the same loving wish to yourself, saying *May I be happy.*

Maybe the feelings of love and kindness you are having now seem small and hard to notice. Or maybe they feel very powerful and intense. *However it is, is fine.* There is no need for things to be different.

Breathe and stretch into the practice of sending and receiving kindness and love.

In the last few minutes of this practice, you can experiment with offering loving-kindness to people you love, to people you have never met, and to people you find it difficult to love or even to like. You can also try sending love to parts of yourself you dislike—like your frizzy hair, your slow reading, or your powerful anger: *May my ex-best friend be happy. May my anger be peaceful and at ease.*

Play with whom and what you send love to. Experiment with the phrases. Find what works best for you. It is fine if it feels awkward or silly. Give it a try. You might be surprised about what happens when you send caring and kindness to people or to parts of yourself that you dislike.

When you are having a bad day, remember that you can offer yourself the love and kindness you have found here, just by saying *May I be happy* silently to yourself.

Do this loving-kindness practice as often as you wish.

Let it remind you that you are loveable just as you are, and that you can send and receive love whenever you want.

To end this practice, say a couple of phrases for *everyone*:

May everyone be happy.

May everyone be peaceful and at ease.

And a couple of phrases for yourself:

May I be happy, just as I am.

May I be peaceful and at ease, just as I am.

It's okay and completely normal if this practice feels awkward or uncomfortable at first. Hang in there and see what you discover as you continue to practice.

chapter 60

Reflection:
Loving-Kindness

How was the Loving-Kindness practice for you? Again, however it was is absolutely fine.

_____

_____

What feelings and thoughts did you have while practicing?

_____

_____

_____

_____

Did you find it easy or difficult to receive love from others?

Circle one: Easy.   Difficult.   In-between.

Did you find it easy or difficult to send love to others?

Circle one: Easy.   Difficult.   In-between.

Did you find it easy or difficult to send love to yourself?

Circle one: Easy.   Difficult.   In-between.

Did you want to joke about it or blow it off?

Circle one: Yes.   No.   Not sure.

How did your body feel as you practiced?

_____

_____

_____

_____

How is it to know that you can practice sending and receiving love?

_____

_____

Are you willing to play or work with this practice?

Circle one: Yes.   No.   Maybe.

Are you willing to try it with people you find difficult?

Circle one: Yes.   No.   Maybe.

Are you willing to use this practice as an antidote to Unkind Mind?

Circle one: Yes.   No.   Maybe.

giving yourself the gift of mindfulness

Not surprisingly, this week's practice is about bringing mindfulness more fully into your life. Use the mnemonics you find most helpful in supporting your ability to *respond* mindfully to life circumstances (see chapter 58). Also practice sending and receiving love by doing the Loving-Kindness practice. If possible, start small, responding to simple situations and sending love to people in your life who are easy to love. Then step it up a notch, responding to more challenging situations and sending love to more challenging people. Stretch and see if you can strengthen your capacity to respond to and be loving with yourself and others.

* Practice responding rather than reacting to people and events in your life using the ABCs, STAR, and PEACE practices.

* Do the Loving-Kindness practice every day.

Mindfulness is ~

Portable. It moves into your life and into the world.

part 8

the end of the out-breath

In this book, you've learned a lot of skills that can help you respond more mindfully in daily life. Bringing kind and curious attention to yourself, others, and life as it is in the moment gives you the information you need to choose your behavior—in other words, respond rather than react. To summarize, here are the basic elements for practicing mindfulness and being more mindful in your daily life:

* Using the breath to settle into the Still Quiet Place

* Enjoying moments of peace, ease, and happiness

* Noticing when things are difficult

* Bringing your kind and curious attention to thoughts, feelings, and physical sensations

* Considering whether resistance is increasing your suffering

* If other people are involved, considering their thoughts, feelings, and desires

* Choosing a new street rather than falling into a hole

* Responding rather than reacting

* Offering yourself and others loving-kindness

This final part of the book will provide a few more ways of decreasing your suffering and bringing mindfulness and compassion into your day-to-day life. These skills will help you navigate all the moments of your life, including the difficult ones, with more peace, ease, and happiness.

chapter 61

Activity:
Understanding Self-Esteem

Self-esteem is how we think about ourselves. It has two main aspects:

Thinking about ourselves in comparison to others: *I am better than or worse than you.*

Thinking about ourselves in terms of success and failure: *I'm a good (successful) student, athlete, musician, person…*or *I'm a bad (failing) student, athlete, musician, person…*

Self-esteem seems great when we're on the upside—thinking we're better than someone else or feeling successful. But when we're on the downside of self-esteem, it can be like pouring gasoline on the fire of Unkind Mind.

Let's do a little experiment to see how this works. Start by bringing to mind a time when you felt successful or like you were better than someone else. Recall the situation in detail and then briefly describe it here:

_____

_____

What thoughts did you have in the situation?

_____

_____

What feelings did you have in the situation?

_____

_____

How did these thoughts and feelings show up in your body? (If you're not sure, here's a hint: when I feel successful or better than others, I have a bit of swagger, my head is high, and my chest is literally a bit puffed up.)

_____

_____

Now do the same thing with the downside of self-esteem. Bring to mind a time when you felt like a failure or like you were worse than someone else. Recall the situation in detail and then briefly describe it here:

_____

_____

What thoughts did you have in the situation?

_____

_____

What feelings did you have in the situation?

_____

_____

How did these thoughts and feelings show up in your body? (Again, here's a hint: when I feel like a failure or worse than others, my body seems like it's a bit deflated and caved in.)

_____

_____

Now list three traits that give you high self-esteem:

_____

_____

_____

Now consider whether your high self-esteem, or pride related to these traits, has a downside. For example, do you feel stressed out when you don't act, behave, or perform as you or others expect? Here are some examples that may clarify this concept:

Trait: *I am tough.*

Downsides:

Sometimes it's exhausting to be tough.

Sometimes I want to be supported and comforted.

Sometimes my toughness is covering my pain.

Trait: *I am nice.*

Downsides:

I often put other people's needs before my own.

I don't take good care of myself.

I do things I don't want to do.

Every trait has a downside and an upside. What are the downsides of the three traits you listed that give you high self-esteem?

_____

_____

_____

_____

_____

_____

The good news is, it's possible to ride the roller coaster of *better than* versus *worse than* and *success* versus *failure* without taking it all quite so seriously. We can learn to truly enjoy our strengths and successes, and accept our weaknesses and so-called failures, without letting them define who we think we are. We can learn to hold these experiences lightly, with kindness and curiosity. It is helpful to remember that the experiences of feeling better than others or successful, and the experiences of feeling worse than others or like a failure, are all temporary, and none of them define us.

chapter 62

Activity:
Practicing Self-Compassion

Self-compassion is based on the understanding that all human beings, including you, have difficulty, and that all human beings, including you, deserve kindness. Unlike self-esteem, self-compassion doesn't depend on what you think of yourself, your successes or failures, or how you compare to others.

According to Dr. Kristin Neff, a pioneer and expert in the field of self-compassion, there are three parts to self-compassion: mindful awareness, kindness toward yourself, and having an understanding of our common humanity. Hopefully, at this point in the book, it's clear that the Still Quiet Place is all about mindful awareness and kindness! Still, let's consider how Dr. Neff describes those two qualities. To paraphrase, she says that *mindful awareness* means being willing to observe negative thoughts and emotions, with openness and clarity, without either suppressing or indulging them. And she describes *self-kindness* as the cultivation of kindness toward oneself, especially when we suffer, fail, or feel inadequate.

The third element of self-compassion is *understanding our common humanity*—recognizing that suffering and feelings of personal inadequacy are part of the shared human experience. Basically this means *everyone* has times when they feel sad, mad, afraid, upset, jealous, insecure, disappointed; these experiences don't just happen to you and you alone. In other words, we *all* feel bad about ourselves sometimes.

So take a moment now to revisit the previous activity (in chapter 61), and bring to mind the situation you wrote down when you felt like you were worse than someone else or like a failure. Bring this situation to mind and heart. Rest your hand on your chest and say these words:

   It was really rough when _____ [fill in the blank].

Everyone goes through tough times.

In this moment, I offer myself kindness and compassion.

How does it feel to practice being a true friend to yourself in this way?

_____

_____

_____

When you're having a rough time, are you willing to practice offering yourself the same kindness and wisdom you'd give a true friend?

Circle one: Yes.   No.   Maybe.

In your experience, does the Loving-Kindness practice in chapter 59 support you in being more compassionate with yourself?

Circle one: Yes.   No.   Maybe.

According to Dr. Neff, self-compassion doesn't just increase well-being; it also increases resilience, the ability to get through hard times. In fact, her research showed that self-compassion increases college students' ability to deal with academic difficulties. So when you are feeling bad and facing challenges—after breaking up with someone, fighting with your parents, receiving a disappointing grade, playing poorly, blowing an audition—give yourself the gift of self-compassion. Place your hand on your heart (if you wish) and use these simple phrases:

It is really rough when _____ [fill in the blank].

Everyone goes through tough times.

In this moment, I offer myself kindness and compassion.

This is a very simple way to befriend yourself when you're having a rough time. While it is enough to simply say the phrases, the more sincerely you can offer yourself the kindness you would offer a friend, the more powerful the practice will be.

chapter 63

Practice:
Mindfulness in Daily Life

Any activity can be done mindfully: eating, showering, walking, doing chores, talking with people, competing in sports, performing on stage, or even just hanging out with friends. There are lots of benefits to being more mindful during daily activities.

As you have hopefully already discovered, doing an enjoyable activity mindfully almost always allows you to enjoy it more fully; doing an unenjoyable activity mindfully often allows you to decrease your resistance and thus decrease your suffering. Also doing an activity mindfully brings your attention into the present, preventing you from worrying about the future and obsessing about the past, and this decreases both anxiety and depression. And most importantly, as you have learned, bringing mindfulness into difficult situations allows you to respond rather than react, and this often will prevent the difficulty from spiraling out of control. That's why mindfulness is being used in many Fortune 500 companies and police and fire departments, as well as by professional athletes, physicians, lawyers, schoolteachers, musicians, actors, chefs, military personnel, and people in almost every profession.

Doing daily activities mindfully means bringing your full, kind, and curious attention to whatever it is that you're doing. Here's a mindful toothbrushing practice that you can try:

> As you begin to brush your teeth, bring your full, kind, and curious attention to what you're doing. During the few minutes it takes to brush your teeth, see if you can give your complete attention to this activity and nothing else—not homework, a problem you had during the day, an exciting event that's coming up, texting a friend... Simply rest your attention on brushing your teeth, here and now.

Feel yourself pick up the toothpaste and unscrew the cap. Feel the texture and temperature of the tube and the cap. Feel yourself pick up the toothbrush, squeeze the toothpaste, and put down the toothpaste. Feel the movement of your hand, arm, tongue, and cheeks as you brush your teeth. Notice the taste of the toothpaste and whether you choose to spit or swallow.

If you notice that your mind wanders into the future or the past, that's okay. It happens to everyone. In fact, noticing this means you're being mindful! So when you realize that your attention has wandered, gently bring it back to the sensations of brushing, the flavor of the toothpaste, and even the scent. Listen to the sounds of brushing your teeth and to the sound of the water as you rinse your toothbrush. Feel your movements as you put the toothbrush and toothpaste away.

Again, *any* activity can be done mindfully; so you may want to play with mindful walking, showering, resting…

chapter 64

Practice:
Flashlight

This practice combines many of the basic practices offered in earlier chapters into one simple form. You can read through the following passage and then give the practice a try on your own, or you can find a recorded version on my CD, *Still Quiet Place: Mindfulness for Teens*, available through iTunes and Amazon. Find a relatively quiet, private place to practice and make yourself comfortable.

> When you're ready, settle in and close your eyes. Then rest the flashlight of your attention on your breath and the Still Quiet Place between the breaths…
>
> After a minute or so, gently shine the flashlight of your attention on sound, listening to sounds in the room, sounds beyond the room, and even sounds in your body—your breath, your heartbeat, a ringing in your ears…
>
> In your own time, shine the flashlight of attention on your body, noting where your body makes contact with the chair or the bed, your clothing, and the air, noting areas that feel comfortable or uncomfortable…
>
> Again, whenever you're ready, shine the flashlight of attention on thoughts, noticing thoughts as they come and go…
>
> In your own time, shine the flashlight of attention on emotions, simply acknowledging whatever you're feeling in the moment…
>
> Now, shine the flashlight of attention on the breath, and then on the Still Quiet Place itself… Just breathing and resting in stillness and quietness…

It can be very helpful to know that we have a flashlight of attention, and that with practice we can learn to turn it on and choose where to focus it. We can expand the beam of our attention to include everything, or we can narrow it to just one thing: the ball and the hoop, a test question, the person in front of us, the taste of a tangerine… This ability to expand and narrow the flashlight of our attention is very helpful in many situations: when playing a sport or a musical instrument, while taking a test, during a difficult conversation—the list goes on.

chapter 65

Activity:
Letter to a Friend

At the end of every Still Quiet Place course, I invite participants to write a letter to a friend describing what the course has meant to them. The friend can be anyone, even a pet or an imaginary friend. Now, I invite you to do the same. Since this is mindfulness and not English class, you can just write whatever is true for you, without worrying about spelling or punctuation. Your letter can be anonymous, and you don't need to send it unless you want to. It is just a simple way for you to reflect on your experience. And if you'd like, you may share your letter with me by sending it to me at dramy@stillquietplace.com, using "letter to a friend" as the subject line.

When you're ready, write a brief letter to a friend who knows nothing about mindfulness. In your letter, describe:

* How it feels to rest in the Still Quiet Place, or awareness

* How you've used mindfulness in your daily life

Dear _____,

_____

_____

_____

_____

_____

_____

_____

_____

_____

_____

_____

_____

_____

Sincerely,

_____

continuing to give yourself the gift of mindfulness

By doing the practices and engaging with the concepts in this book, you have truly given yourself an invaluable gift. You have learned essential skills that will benefit you in every area of your life—at home, at school, in sports and performing arts, at work, and, most importantly, in your relationships with yourself and others. Almost all people who learn mindfulness as adults (including me) wish that they had learned it when they were younger, because they have found it has improved every area of their lives. They recognize how helpful it would have been to learn these practices as teens and use them during high school, college, and beyond. So I encourage you to really *celebrate* that you have chosen to learn these skills now, and to continue giving yourself, and fully receiving, the gift of mindfulness by maintaining your practice.

Like any other skill, mindfulness fades if we don't use it fairly consistently. Since you won't have reminders from me to help keep you on track with your practice, I encourage you to create some structure for yourself. And of course, if you stop practicing (which most people do), then whenever you realize that you've stopped, you can simply and kindly return to the practice, just like you return your attention to the breath when your mind has wandered. Here are some suggestions for continuing to give yourself the gift of mindfulness:

* Practice mindfulness in daily life.

* For formal practice, use the downloadable guided audio or additional tracks from the CD *Still Quiet Place: Mindfulness for Teens,* and play with a mindfulness timer app, like Insight Timer, which allows you to set a timer for a specific length of time and have chimes sound at various intervals to help you return your attention to the moment.

* Make a promise to yourself to practice for a certain number of minutes a certain number of times per week. Choose how long and how often, and

try to stick to it. Put a reminder on your calendar or phone for one month from now. Then, when that time arrives, with kindness and curiosity, check in and see if you have kept your promise to yourself. If you have kept your promise, choose whether you want to continue practicing. If you haven't kept your promise, choose whether you want to begin practicing again.

Mindfulness is ~
Yours: your practice to help you live with peace and happiness.

Congrats Again!

Congratulations! By working with this book, you've given yourself the precious gift of mindfulness. You've practiced bringing kind and curious attention to the moments of your life, and in the process, you've developed skills for creating a less stressful and more enjoyable world for yourself and others. I'm so happy that you've learned these skills.

I hope you feel that you've become a better friend to yourself, and that in some way you and I have become friends. If you'd like to share your experience with me, or if you have any questions or suggestions, please e-mail me at dramy@stillquietplace .com.

May your mindfulness practice support you in choosing wise and kind actions and in living a peaceful and joyful life.

Appendix

Nine Dots Puzzle Solution

The most common solution to the puzzle appears below. In this example, the first line begins on the top left dot, goes straight down *beyond* the lower left dot. The second line goes diagonally to the right through the lower middle dot, *beyond* the middle dot on the right aligning to the right of the top dot on the right. The third line goes to the top left dot, and the fourth line goes diagonally down to the bottom right dot. Expanding the possibilities further, it is useful to note that there are actually four variations of the solution—one beginning in each corner—meaning more than one right answer.

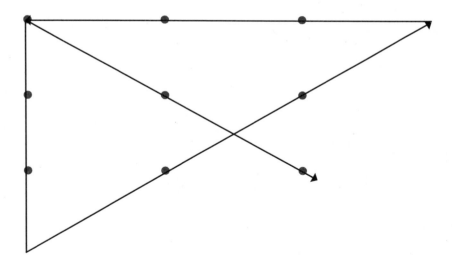

As mentioned previously, you can see that the solutions require thinking outside the box.

Amy Saltzman, MD, is a holistic physician, mindfulness coach, scientist, wife, mother, devoted student of transformation, longtime athlete, and occasional poet. Her passion is supporting people of all ages in enhancing their well-being and discovering *A Still Quiet Place* within. She is recognized by her peers as a visionary and pioneer in the fields of holistic medicine and mindfulness for youth. She is founder and director of the Association for Mindfulness in Education, an inaugural and longstanding member of the steering committee for the Mindfulness in Education Network, and a founding member of the Northern California Advisory Committee on Mindfulness. She lives in the San Francisco Bay Area with her husband and two teenaged children. For more information, visit http://www.stillquietplace.com.

More ⏱ Instant Help Books for Teens

An Imprint of New Harbinger Publications

THE STRESS REDUCTION WORKBOOK FOR TEENS

Mindfulness Skills to Help You Deal with Stress

ISBN: 978-1572246973 / US $15.95

THE TEEN GIRL'S SURVIVAL GUIDE

Ten Tips for Making Friends, Avoiding Drama & Coping with Social Stress

ISBN: 978-1626253063 / US $16.95

THE ANXIETY SURVIVAL GUIDE FOR TEENS

CBT Skills to Overcome Fear, Worry & Panic

ISBN: 978-1626252431 / US $16.95

DON'T LET YOUR EMOTIONS RUN YOUR LIFE FOR TEENS

Dialectical Behavior Therapy Skills for Helping You Manage Mood Swings, Control Angry Outbursts & Get Along with Others

ISBN: 978-1572248830 / US $16.95

THINK CONFIDENT, BE CONFIDENT FOR TEENS

A Cognitive Therapy Guide to Overcoming Self-Doubt & Creating Unshakable Self-Esteem

ISBN: 978-1608821136 / US $16.95

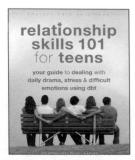

RELATIONSHIP SKILLS 101 FOR TEENS

Your Guide to Dealing with Daily Drama, Stress, & Difficult Emotions Using DBT

ISBN: 978-1626250529 / US $16.95

newharbingerpublications
1-800-748-6273 / newharbinger.com

(VISA, MC, AMEX / prices subject to change without notice)

Follow Us

Don't miss out on new books in the subjects that interest you.
Sign up for our **Book Alerts** at **newharbinger.com/bookalerts**

Register your **new harbinger** titles for additional benefits!

When you register your **new harbinger** title—purchased in any format, from any source—you get access to benefits like the following:

- Downloadable accessories like printable worksheets and extra content
- Instructional videos and audio files
- Information about updates, corrections, and new editions

Not every title has accessories, but we're adding new material all the time.

Access free accessories in 3 easy steps:

1. Sign in at NewHarbinger.com (or **register** to create an account).

2. Click on **register a book**. Search for your title and click the **register** button when it appears.

3. Click on the **book cover or title** to go to its details page. Click on **accessories** to view and access files.

That's all there is to it!

If you need help, visit:

NewHarbinger.com/accessories

new harbinger
CELEBRATING
40 YEARS